MACUMBA

The Teachings of Maria-José, Mother of the Gods

by Serge Bramly

T0204540

City Lights Books
San Francisco

Original French edition © 1975 by Editions Seghers, Paris
English translation © 1977 by St. Martin's Press
First City Lights Edition 1994

10 9 8 7 6 5 4 3 2

All photographs, unless otherwise noted, © Serge Bramly

Cover photograph © Don Klein
Cover design by Rex Ray
Book design by Elaine Katzenberger
Typography by Harvest Graphics

Library of Congress Cataloging-in-Publication Data

Bramly, Serge, 1949-
      Macumba : the teachings of Maria-José, mother of the gods /
by Serge Bramly.
          p.   cm.
      Interviews with Maria-José, a mother of the gods.
      ISBN 0-87286-286-0 (pbk.): $14.95
          1. Macumba (Cult) 2. Maria-José, mae — Interviews.
      3. Brazil — Religion — 20th century. I. Maria-José, mae.
      II. Title.
BL2592.M23B73   1994
299'.67 — dc20   94-290
                                                         CIP

City Lights Books are available to bookstores through our primary
distributor: Subterranean Company. P.O. Box 160, 265 S. 5th St.,
Monroe, OR 97456. 541-847-5274. Toll-free orders 800-274-7826.
FAX 541-847-6018. Our books are also available through library
jobbers and regional distributors. For personal orders and catalogs,
please write to City Lights Books, 261 Columbus Avenue,
San Francisco, CA 94133.

CITY LIGHTS BOOKS are edited by Lawrence Ferlinghetti and
Nancy J. Peters and published at the City Lights Bookstore,
261 Columbus Avenue, San Francisco, CA 94133.

CONTENTS

The author has retained the Brazilian spelling of all proper names. The Brazilian *x* is pronounced "sh"; thus, the words *Xangô*, *Exú*, or *Oxalá* should be prounounced respectively "Shangô," "Eshú," and "Oshalá." *H* before a vowel is equivalent to *y*. Thus, *velho* is read "velyo," and *maconha* should be read "maconya."

The photograph which accompanies the Preface to this new edition was taken during the Festival of Iemanjá on the Copacabana Beach in Rio de Janeiro on December 31, 1990. © Don Klein.

MACUMBA

PREFACE

S ERGE Bramly's book is a great introduction to a little-
known spiritual path. In no way a titillating anthropolog-
ical curiosity, it is an opening to a way of life and belief that is
followed by fifteen million Brazilians as well as millions more
all across the Western hemisphere. Along with its sister religions of Vodun, Santería, and Ifa, Macumba — also known as
Umbanda outside of Rio — worships deities from Africa.
These religions entail complex philosophical concepts and
spiritual discipline, yet are too often ignorantly labeled "prim-
itive" and falsely relegated to a realm of fetish-dominated
superstition.

In the years since Serge Bramly's book came out, the religion has grown greatly — it is appalling that recent books,
which list and discuss goddesses and gods, continue to ignore

the whole spectrum of African deities; the common prejudice against these religions and the people who follow them prevents a profound and rich spiritual tradition from being known and understood.

Racial, political, and economic considerations have everything to do with the acceptance of a religion. When a belief system is denied respect its followers are denied power. The struggle for legalization of important religions of African origin has been a long one; challenges from Fundamentalists who call all other forms of worship "Deviltry" continue today. It's time to broaden the perspective: there are more Macumbeiros than Mormons. Freedom of religion must be recognized as a universal human right; unrestricted personal spiritual choice is a precondition for honorable interaction between peoples.

The strength and beauty of Macumba and its sister religions come directly from the sophisticated structure of the mother-religion in Africa: this essence is externalized in the ritual form of the music and dance — the divine interaction between humans and Living Gods — and internalized in the spiritual regeneration of its devotees.

The most ancient African roots may be found in the social, political, and religious structures of the extraordinary culture of the African city-states of western Nigeria when the Yoruba civilization was in its Renaissance about 1000-1500 common era. Then, about 1700 C.E. the Yorubas were weakened by internal warfare and by external raids by the Dahomey and Fulani peoples; as a result of these conflicts around the Gulf of Guinea (from West and Central Western Africa: Benin, Nigeria, Cameroon, Gabon, Congo, Zaire, Angola) the human fallout was sold to an eager market of European slave-traders waiting on the coast.

More than one third of all the slaves in the Americas landed in Brazil, carrying with them highly sophisticated religious traditions and making Brazil the second largest African nation in the world. The harrowing displacement to a distant continent and the horrifying conditions of slavery brought people together who had different deity paths yet shared a very similar religious outlook; perhaps for the first time in their history they pooled their religious knowledge, laying the foundation for the various ways of Orixa worship we have today.

Macumba is much more than simply a transplanted regional, cultural or spiritual tradition. The primary Gods were born in Africa; along with 3.5 million African slaves, they survived the Middle Passage to Brazil, where they have been reborn and continue to be reborn, the same, yet different. In Brazil and beyond, every degree of fusion between cultural social and racial traditions can be found: from strongly African in the Bahia African-Pride Movement of the Afro-blocos, Candomblé, Batuque, to the most westernized, Umbanda.

Macumba's formal beginnings were a typically Brazilian reaction against the practices of the narrow all-white pantheon which the Spiritists popularized in the early years of this century. Instead of honoring only the "revealed" deities of the major religions that are based upon written authority, Umbanda incorporated previously secret African deities as well as indigenous native practices: not only the Orixas but also the Preto Velhos (the old slave ancestors) are welcomed, and particular honor is paid to the local spirits, the Caboclos. Western Magical traditions of Spiritism, Kardecism and Kabbalah are continually elaborated and modified.

Because the historical record is unreliable (slaves were often listed simply as "from Guinea") it is difficult to get accurate information about the origins of the African populace — tracing the course of the survival or extinction of the worship of certain deities is equally challenging. Regional history made for noticeable differences between Macumba and the other Orixa-worshiping religions — an obvious example is that of Pombagira. The sacred harlot and wife of Exú, the magical gatekeeper, Pombagira is Goddess of the Crossroads, an important deity/archetype in Brazil, seldom worshiped elsewhere. Research indicates Pombagira may have come to Brazil as part of Kongo tradition — "mpambu nzila," roads crossing — perhaps her devotees did not survive in other areas.

Much depended (and still depends) upon the capability of any surviving devotees to pass their knowledge on to others — and how well their beliefs and ritual forms fit the new situation. Macumba prides itself on being well-adapted to modern life and on using verifiable psychic skills. Umbanda is a very practical religion: if something works it continues as part of the worship, if something doesn't bring results, it may well be dropped.

The closer any religion comes to answering the need we have for understanding our relationship with all beings, the more easily it transcends cultural barriers. Spirituality travels around: essential ideas coagulate in one place, then move on, mutating as they develop among different peoples. Like every great religion, Macumba's ability to transform both itself and its followers isn't restricted or specific to one place, race, or time.

This book is a landmark — for many of us it was the first

respectful work we found in print about Macumba, and it was a welcome introduction to a marvelous Mother of the Gods, Maria José. Macumba is spreading well beyond the boundaries of Brazil, many more people of all races practice the faith, charity and good humor essential to Orixa worship, and there are even more people devoted to the Living Gods. We hope the perception of the drumbeat-heartbeat of the universe continues to deepen and expand — SARAVÁ UMBANDA!

EXÚ YANGI, HERE IS YOUR BOOK. WE HOPE YOU ARE PLEASED. AXÉ.

Renée Pinzón and Sin Soracco
1994

CASA SÃO JERÔNIMO

ARTIGOS PARA RITUAIS DE:

Umbanda - Quimbanda e
Candomblé, por preços
sem competidores

Aceitamos encomendas – Veja e Comprove
Até às 20 Horas

Advertisement for the "Casa São Jeronimo," a shop selling articles for
Umbanda, Quimbanda (Black Magic), and Candomblé.

INTRODUCTION

W HEN I was first in Brazil, whenever I asked about the lighted candles placed at night at downtown intersections or in front of modern office buildings, I invariably received only the most evasive answers, accompanied by amused or embarrassed smiles.

One day I found two decapitated statuettes beneath a tree. I wanted to pick them up in order to examine them more closely, but a friend intervened. "It's dangerous. You mustn't touch that sort of thing," he told me. When I pressed him for more information he claimed to know nothing further on the subject.

One evening I accidentally stepped on a rice-filled terra cotta platter which had been left on the ground. My companion turned pale, whispering that I had just committed a serious offense. He made me promise to redeem myself by lighting an all-night candle. Despite my insistent questions, I could learn no more. "They are Macumba offerings, *despachos*. You mustn't get involved," I was told. "It's just a bunch of idle superstitions. . . ." But my friend telephoned me later on that evening to make sure that I had followed his instructions.

Brazilians are reluctant to talk about Macumba. They either deny its existence or pretend to be above it. Only rarely do they admit to practicing it. They prefer to think of it as an outmoded legacy from the past, which can be happily consigned to the category of national folklore.

They attribute it to the most illiterate members of Brazilian society. Macumba, they say, is the religion of the old black slaves who were brought to work Brazil's plantations between the sixteenth and nineteenth centuries. They call it a corrupted version of African animism; a naive, chaotic hotch-potch of superstitions and beliefs which, as they would have it, survived in Brazil as a form of opposition to the religion of the masters during the long period of slavery. As to its current practice, they view it as an antiquated effort on the part of blacks to preserve their integrity, a kind of blind sustenance in adversity.

Nevertheless, Macumba is omnipresent in Brazil. It is a constant source of inspiration for popular songs and Carnival sambas. Each of its major holidays (January 1st, May 13th, etc.) is the object of special magazine and television coverage. There are a number of radio stations that broadcast only Macumba's sacred songs on designated evenings. Both literature and film also draw a number of their themes from Macumba. The great Bahian writer Jorge Amado, for example (*Doña Flor and Her Two Husbands, Gabriela, Clove, and*

Cinnamon), who is proud of his adherence to a Macumba center (he is *Obá* of Xangô, of the *terreiro* of the Gantois), has made it the central theme of his work. Macumba has so thoroughly penetrated Brazilian culture that some of its expressions — often of African origin — have become an accepted part of everyday speech.

During the past few years numerous attempts have been made to obtain an exact figure on the number of Macumba centers in the various states of Brazil. The monthly *Manchette* (May 1976) speaks in terms of forty thousand centers in Rio de Janeiro and the state of Guanabara. There are close to sixteen thousand centers in São Paulo and eighteen thousand in Rio Grande do Sul. On December 31, 1975, in Rio de Janeiro alone, the number of people taking part in the festival of the goddess Iemanjá was estimated at nearly a million.

The city of San Salvador (capital of the state of Bahia) has three hundred sixty-five churches (one for every day of the year) and nearly four thousand centers of Afro-Brazilian sects, of which two thousand have been officially counted. Despite the rapid progress of electrification, the sale of candles in the city is steadily increasing, a phenomenon which is perhaps unique in the entire world. I was unable to find a single person there who was willing to pick up one of the hundreds of offerings which line the beaches every night.

Early in 1972 I attended a number of Macumba ceremonies in cities throughout Brazil. While I was everywhere received with the same friendliness and warmth, I was never allowed to forget that I was a foreigner — a *gringo*. And while I was able to observe certain common features, certain unvarying characteristics and certain constants, I was stuck too by the disparity, the diversity and the lack of organization between the different centers. The religious calendar, rites and vocabulary differ from center to center. Even the name of the cult is not the same from state to state. The word Macumba is actually used only in the state of Rio de Janeiro, and believers generally employ the word *Umbanda*. In the northeast, in Pernambuco for example, they say *Xangô* or *Catimbó*. In Bahia *Candomblé* is the term used, with its own special variant: the *Candomblé of Caboclo*. In the south one hears *Batuque* or the Cult of the Nations (*Culto de Nação*). In the Amazon the word *Pajelança* is employed.

In order to penetrate, to better understand what we might call, for lack of a better word, Macumba or the Afro-Brazilian religions, I began to collect a great quantity of literature. There must be about a hundred volumes on the subject in Brazil. Certain excellent works, such as that of Nina Rodriguez, while of indisputable ethnological value, offer only an outsider's impressions of aspects of the cult which all too often belong already to the past. Others on the other hand, such as that of Tancredo da Silva Pinto (sometimes called the "Black Pope of Brazil"), while written directly by disciples and initiates of the cult, fail, either out of naiveté or because they were written for a specialized audience already well acquainted with the subject. They present detailed aspects of the cults without ever giving adequate descriptions of the whole.

Seeing my efforts to understand the complex teachings of Macumba, a friend revealed to me in the course of a casual conversation that he was a member of a Macumba center. I besieged him with questions. He claimed that his first meeting with the *Mae de Santo,*[1] the "Great Priestess" of this center, had been one of the decisive moments of his life, and he promised to introduce me to her.

I told him of my other friends' reluctance to discuss the subject. "Here no one likes to admit to practicing Macumba," he explained to me. "Since Macumba does not take place on a visible level, its action cannot be observed. It reveals itself only in results. It has no solid scientific base. That is why most people prefer to deny its existence rather than expose themselves to ridicule for believing in things which science disputes. But all Brazilians have at least one Macumba story up their sleeves, and you would be astonished to learn how many people keep candles and amulets hidden in their dressers."

I asked him how many Brazilians he thought were followers of Macumba. He began to laugh. "But all Brazilians are *macumbeiros* from birth! It would be impossible to give you an exact number, even an estimate. There are those who regularly attend a center, a *terreiro*, and those who have recourse to Macumba only once or twice in their whole life. There are also those who are afraid of it, but that too is a way of believing. Personally, I don't know anyone who wouldn't fit into at least one of these three categories."

"What does the word Macumba mean?"

"Macumba is a general term. Originally it meant the place where the black slaves performed their rites. Today, particularly in the state of Rio, it is used to designate all the different Afro-Brazilian sects. It can mean the act of sacrificing to the gods ('to do a Macumba' or 'do a work of Macumba'), the place

[1]Mae de Santo, or its masculine counterpart, Pae de Santo, is literally Mother of Saint (or Father of Saint). But in fact the saints of Macumba are African gods disguised as Catholic saints simply for reasons of convenience. "Mother of the Gods" therefore seems to me a more correct translation of this term.

of worship ('to go to a Macumba'), the rites which are celebrated in such a place, or simply the cult itself. Because Macumba is the product of a rich and complicated syncretism, it has many different forms. In each area of Brazil a particular influence is dominant, giving the cult its unique regional characteristics.

"The black slaves who introduced the cult to Brazil were from many different areas up and down the eastern coast of Africa. There were Dahomians, Congolese, Fons, Angolans, and Geges. Once they were freed the former slaves regrouped into these original nations, each of which had had its own religion. With time all these cults have more or less grown together into one. But there are still differences between, for example, a Bantu center and a Nago one.

"However, the most traditional centers are now on their way out, and their place is being taken by growing numbers of Umbanda centers. Umbanda draws on many different sources. It incorporates Christian elements into the African rituals and appropriates all the mystics it has heard of. It also practices spiritism.

"Then there is Quimbanda, black magic. . . . But there are no clearly defined boundaries between all the various forms of Afro-Brazilian religion. That's why, for simplicity's sake, they are generally referred to as Macumba. You see, the different centers have little contact with each other. From one terreiro to the next the gods may have different names and different functions. The rituals are different, and even the myths may be at variance. Although Macumba is legally recognized, it is not very institutionalized. However, all its forms share a common base.

"The terreiro to which I belong, for example, follows the

Umbandist line. But this classification doesn't mean too much. In practice my terreiro, like many others, goes way beyond simple Umbanda. In its organizational structure, its physical layout and in many of its rituals, it is related also to Candomblé, which is more traditional (African). Perhaps this is because the Mother who runs it is from Bahia, the territory of Candomblé. I think the personality of the Mae de Santo or Pae de Santo gives a terreiro its individual stamp."

I wanted to know what had first attracted him to Macumba, what had led him to go to a terreiro.

"I began to go to Maria-José's terreiro — she is the Mother to whom I will introduce you — about four years ago. I had never really been interested in Macumba before that. I was in analysis at the time, and had been for many years. From our very first encounter Maria-José was able to pinpoint the exact source of my problems. She told me that part of me was being suffocated, that I existed only partially, and that if I kept up like that I would never understand myself, never come to know my true personality. I returned to see her. She began to perform for me what she calls a 'work.' It would be hard for me to describe just how her system works. I think a genuine psychological process lies beneath the rituals, which at first seem meaningless. In any case, I stopped seeing my analyst. My life changed. At the moment I'm discovering a whole part of myself I was previously unaware of."

This sounded too simple to me. I asked him to be more specific. Was there a particular treatment? What exactly did he mean by "work"? How could he equate a session of analysis with a Macumba ceremony?

He shrugged his shoulders. "I don't know. It's as if everything took place without my knowledge. When I first attend-ed the ceremonies I was very skeptical. I didn't really think the Mother would be able to do much for me. But there's some-thing very reassuring about the atmosphere of a terreiro. Perhaps I returned those first few times simply for the pleasure of it. To listen to the drums, watch the dancers, smell the incense. . . .

"No, there is no real treatment as such. The Mother gave me her blessing, rubbed me with herbs and instructed me about certain small offerings to be put in specific places. This is what she calls a 'work': to perform a ritual, light a candle, pronounce certain words or sacrifice to a god (*santo*). All this can seem a bit ridiculous. The Mother talks about faith and charity. There's nothing very elevated in her conversation; in fact, at times it sounds exactly like a catechism. But little by little it's as if some charm were working; you feel stronger, surer, about facing life. Macumba is like a powerful family which protects you, which is always there, always present, and in whose heart you have a place. You no longer feel abandoned or alone. Things become simpler, more obvious. And soon, absurd as it may seem, everything begins to go better: work, romantic or psychological problems, everything improves or is resolved. My financial situation, my family problems . . . you can't just call it magic. There is no explanation. All you can do is observe what happens. . . . It would be better for you to see it with your own eyes."

I met Mother Maria-José one week later at her center, on the occasion of a celebration in honor of the god Xangô. From that point on I was to see her regularly for several years.

It was not my intention at the outset to undertake a lengthy study. I simply hoped to gather information which would help me understand the complicated symbolism of the ceremonies I attended. In the course of a conversation I would ask a few questions and Maria-José would reply with generous indulgence. Sometimes she received me in her bedroom; more often we would meet in the terreiro kitchen, which was always the center of a whirl of activity. She spoke with humor of her gods, as if they were familiar friends. At times she anticipated my questions, laughing at my foreigner's ignorance. She expressed herself in a lofty Portuguese, with a certain grandeur and unfailing kindness.

At the end of a year I noticed a common thread to all our loosely-structured conversations. I collected all my notes and put them in order. To make them more accessible I arranged them into four continuous interviews. I recorded most of our discussions afterwards from memory. Nonetheless, I have attempted wherever possible to reproduce Maria-José's intonation and way of speaking.

This book does not pretend to present a complete analysis of Macumba, but simply to trace the thinking of a single Mother of the Gods.

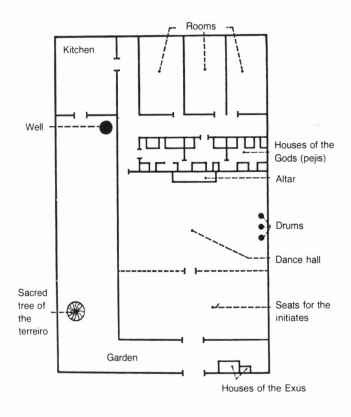

Layout of a terreiro.

THE DESCENT OF THE GODS

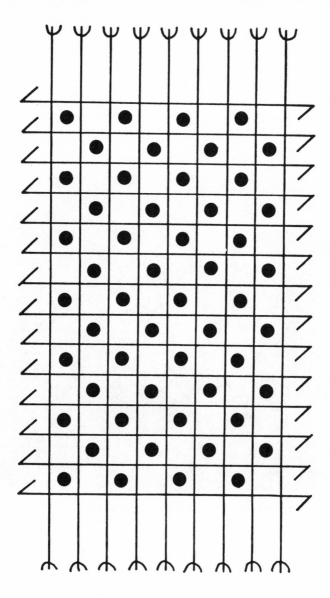

Graphic Invocation of Exú:
Exú Marabo

Defumaçao or fumigation of the terreiro, before a ceremony.

The altar of the gods in the ceremonial hall of Maria-José's terreiro.

Entrance of the drummers.

Entrance of the mediums.

The ritual salute.

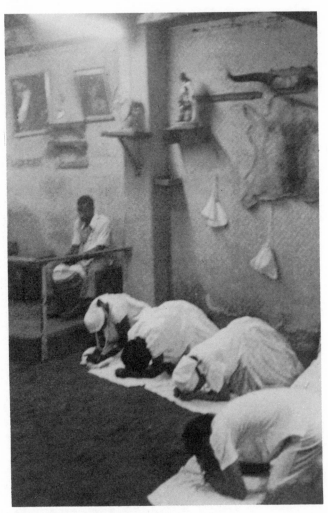

Greetings from the mediums.

The warrior god Ogum appears, armed and helmeted, sprinkling the
faithful with sugar cane liquor.

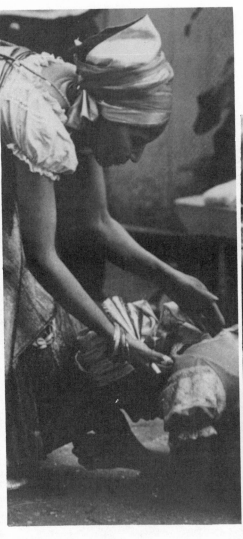

Greeting to the Mother of the Gods.

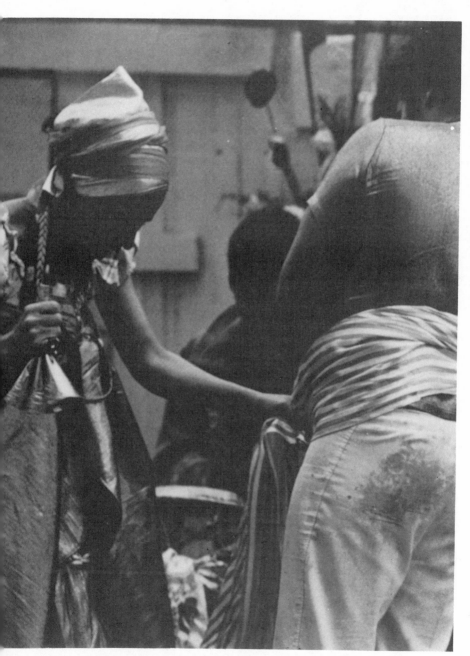

Ringing the agogô, the ritual metal bell, to summon the gods.

The drums "call" the gods.

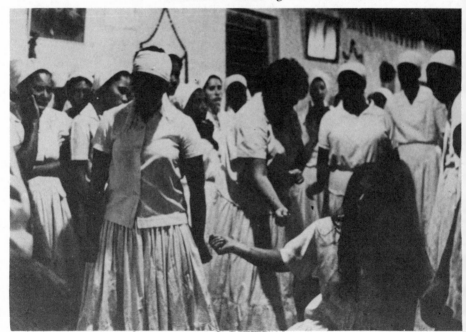

The beginning of the trance.

First signs of the trance: with empty eyes, a medium hops in place
amid a circle of initiates.

Mediums possessed by pretos velhos, old black people.

Lighting the pipe of a medium who is possessed by the spirit of a preto velho.

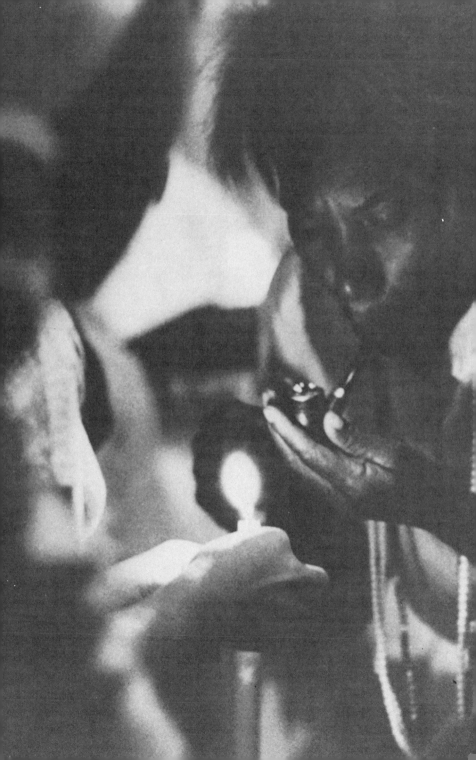

Dancers inside the terreiro.

Dancing.

The gods descend.

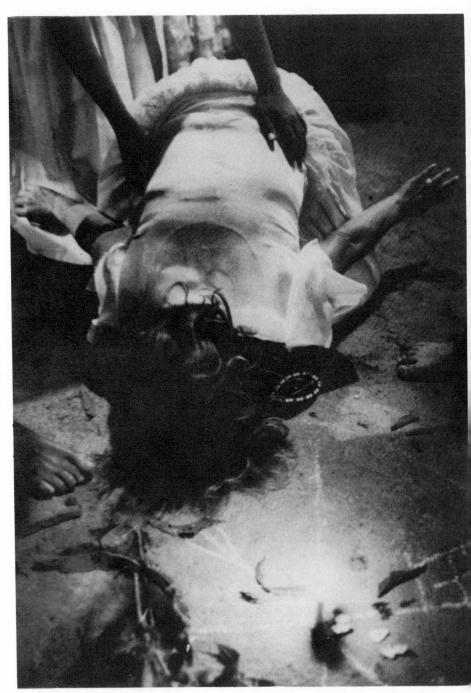

A medium in a trance salutes a magic diagram, a ponto riscado, on the floor of the ceremonial hall.

THE DESCENT OF THE GODS

THE smell of incense, candles and fresh-cut leaves . . . The walls, which have been papered with an odd design in pale blue and white, are covered with religious figures (Christ, Saint George slaying the dragon, etc.) rosaries and hand lettered signs — No Smoking, Respect the Law of Umbanda. The roof beams are hidden by a false ceiling made of thousands of tiny colored paper flags strung on thread. Here and there throughout the room candles burn in the sultry air. Outside, night is falling.

The large rectangular room is divided in two by a low, narrow barrier with an opening at the center. On one side of this divide the spectators, the faithful who have come to seek the help of Umbanda's gods, sit on long wooden benches — fifty-odd people of all ages and classes.

On the other side are the initiates — the mediums, "sons and daughters of the gods." The daughters of the gods are dressed in their ceremonial costumes: long pleated satin or cotton skirts, either white or blue, under which lie many layers of elaborate petticoats; puff-sleeved blouses appliquéd with lace; and innumerable glass bead necklaces in which are often entangled crosses or tin medallions. Immaculate white scarves have been wrapped around their heads like turbans. The mediums walk barefoot on the packed-earth floor, which has been strewn with green leaves.

At the far end of the room there is an altar with figures of saints, plaster statuettes, vases of flowers, candles, satin, ribbons, a crystal bowl, chipped glasses filled with clear water, flasks of perfume, a crucifix, and a large box of cigars. In a niche to the right of the altar there is a large grey mass — the vertebra of a whale.

The Brazilian friend who has invited me to attend the meeting leads me through the opening in the small room divider. I take off my sandals. I am introduced to the Mother of the Gods. Mother Maria-José is about fifty years old. Her features are delicate and energetic. She watches me with an amused curiosity. She is wearing the white ceremonial costume. After the usual polite exchange of formalities she welcomes me, saying that she is flattered to receive a foreigner in her terreiro. She asks that a chair be brought for me and sets me up in a corner near the altar, in the place of honor. And then she forgets all about me.

It is eight-thirty. Three men in shirts and pants, each carrying a drum, enter the room. The drums are long and cylindrical, narrow at the bottom and gaudily painted with bright colors.

The Mother comes and goes, speaking to each member of the congregation. She is giving her final instructions. The initiates line up along the walls, each holding a lighted candle. A drumroll is heard. The Mother's assistant, a man with a greying moustache, raises his arms to the sky; he is greeting the audience. He thanks his "Brothers and Sisters in Oxalá" for coming in such numbers. The initiates then pass before the Mother to make the ritual greeting of Umbanda with its theatrical, exaggerated gestures: the double accolade and then the handshake, elbows raised to the level of the head. "Saravá," they say, throwing themselves flat on their stomachs at her feet. She coldly helps them up. Then they greet one another. The ceremony has begun.

The voice of the assistant grows louder. Silence reigns over the audience. He prays:

> I greet the Ways of Umbanda,
> Saravá[1] Ogum, Iemanjá,
> Saravá Oxossi,
> Xangô and Oxalá![2]
> I salute the Ways of Quimbanda,
> the ways of the East,
> the Caboclos and the Pretos Velhos,
> I greet Exú and his family,
> and the family of souls,
> Saravá![3]

[1]Saravá: ritual expression of greeting.

[2]Ogum, Iemanjá, Oxossi, Xangô and Oxalá: names of gods.

[3]The greeting is very important in Afro-Brazilian religions. Before a ceremony is begun, the faithful first greet all the gods and then each other. Each terreiro has its own particular gestures and expressions of greeting.

Everyone applauds. The drums begin to speak. The atmosphere changes imperceptibly. The Mother's assistant, who plays the part of Master of Ceremonies, calls out a name. He is summoning a god. The mediums and initiates sing to the glory of the god who has been named. They shift their weight from one foot to the other in time to the music. The songs are short — two or three stanzas. At the end of each song there is a burst of applause. The assistant summons another god. After a measure's rest the three drums launch a different rhythm and new songs begin.

Complicated diagrams are traced on the floor: words, flags and arrows overlap. The drawings are circular, and a lighted candle is placed in the center of each one.

The dancers brace themselves. Their feet move faster and faster. They assemble in a circle around the Mother, who remains immobile in the center of the room. Her eyes are half-closed, and she seems to be looking at nothing.

She rests her weight on a knotted cane and smokes a broad pipe. The mediums dance and sing around her. They spin in the flickering light of the candles, turning endlessly as the beat accelerates. They summon the gods of Africa, imploring them with all their might to come quickly. Bending very low before the designs which have been traced into the earthen floor before the altar, they lament.

Suddenly a woman separates herself from the circle of dancers. Her turban poorly hides her blond hair. She gives a sharp cry, trembles, and nearly falls. She seems to be dizzy, and her eyes are upturned. The drums do not stop beating. She spins in the center of the room, her white skirt flying about her. She shouts again, and falls in ecstasy on one of the designs on the floor. All her limbs are shaking. The Mother comes toward her slowly and calmly. She picks her up and blows a pipeful of smoke in her face. She calms her by mumbling a prayer.

But from the other side of the room another woman advances. She has removed her turban, and her kinky hair seems to be standing on end. She is doubled over, and leans on a cane striped like a barber's sign. She drags herself along, muttering incomprehensible syllables. She is smoking a seasoned pipe. A bit of saliva shows at the corner of her lips. She breathes heavily. She walks right in front of me. Her voice is broken like the voice of an old man. Little by little almost all the mediums leave the ranks of the singers to dance in the center space of the terreiro. A man dances, gesticulating like a disjointed puppet: he laughs derisively, his head thrown back. A fat black woman with a thick cigar is drinking from the neck of a bottle of *cachaça* — 50% sugar-cane liquor. She puts the bottle down in a corner and stands squarely, ready to greet all her companions. She grabs them around the waist and bluntly gives them the double hug. Then she blows a puff of her cigar smoke in their faces.

A man has fallen to the floor, nervous spasms rocking his whole body. The Mother picks him up and orders the musicians to change their rhythm. She slowly calms him down.

A woman in a trance leaves the ceremonial room through a small door hidden behind a curtain. She returns within seconds wearing a blue satin cape and an aluminum helmet that resembles a child's gladiator hat. She is carrying a large sword. She gives out blood-curdling shrieks and threatens everybody with her weapon.

Hands crossed behind her back, a young woman jumps up and down in place, rolling her eyes. A dancer accidentally bumps into her, but she doesn't even notice. Eyes open, she sees nothing: her mind is elsewhere. Suddenly her whole body goes limp and she bursts out laughing, her arms beating the air like the blades of a windmill. She mimes a strange dialogue. Not a sound can be heard; she is talking to an invisible other, punctuating her words with large, dramatic gestures.

At ten-thirty, on a signal from the Mother, the musicians stop playing. They exit with their drums. The singing continues. The mediums keep the beat by clapping their hands. About fifteen mediums are in a trance. Now they seem calmer. The Mother goes from one to the other, watching them, speaking to them. She whispers something to her assistant, after which he approaches the spectators and announces that the mediums are "ready to receive." One by one he ushers in all those who have come for help (requesting them first to remove their shoes), and guides them each to a different medium.

The woman with the cigar has sat down on the floor very close to me. Once again she has the bottle of cachaça in her hand. As she drinks, the liquor dribbles down her chin. A young, thin, athletic, well-dressed man is led up to her. He approaches timidly. He leans over and whispers at length into her ear. He is explaining his case. She pulls on her cigar, her eyes staring into nothingness. From time to time she asks a question, and he replies with embarrassment. She rises with surprising agility, takes his hands in her own and, without removing the cigar from her mouth, murmurs a prayer. Then she drops his hand and steps back. She walks toward him again, and strokes his face with her fingertips. She is like a hypnotist putting a patient to sleep. A few more magnetic moves and she begins to blow cigar smoke on him; first on his neck, then his shoulders, then his thighs. Finally she pronounces several sentences having to do with candles and red ribbons. The consultation is over. The young man leaves.

The same scene is repeated throughout the room. Those who have come seeking help recount their stories, the mediums perform a few steps and give their recommendations or prescribe a treatment to be followed. When all the visitors have left the Mother gathers the mediums around her. The songs and dancing are resumed (this time without the drums). The dancers are quieter now. The effects of the trance begin to wear off. The ceremony is over when all the mediums have returned to a normal state.

The Mother seems surprised to see that I am still there. "Didn't you leave with everyone else?" she asks. She looks at me with amusement. "Did you like the ceremony?" And, without giving me a chance to reply, she invites me for a *cafesinho*, a small cup of strong, heavily sweetened coffee.

She parts a curtain and I follow her inside the terreiro. The building is much larger than it appears from the outside. We walk down a corridor, she opens a door and we enter the kitchen, an immense room paved with large stones. A coal stove takes up almost a whole wall. Suspended from the ceiling is a smoke-blackened plank from which hang fruits, vegetables, colored glass bottles and potbellied casseroles. In the center of the room is a table with a Formica top. The paint is peeling off the walls, but everything is meticulously clean. A door in the back opens onto a garden. A dog is asleep on the floor.

Water is boiling on the fire. The mediums have changed back into their everyday clothes. The Mother invites me to sit beside her on a stool. She offers me a cup of boiling hot coffee and some cookies.

"Your friend told me that you are interested in our religion. Are you a journalist or professor or one of those things?" My negative reply leaves her perplexed. "But what exactly do you want from me?" I tell her of the changes that my friend had experienced as a result of his initiation into Macumba. I confess that Macumba interests me on a number of levels, and tell her that perhaps with her help I will be able to understand it, if not become a convert. She smiles. "Our religion is at once very simple and very complex. I'm not a very educated woman. I can teach you nothing that you can't see for yourself." And without allowing me to reply she begins to question me, in an exquisitely courteous manner and in pompous and somewhat antiquated language, about my stay in Brazil, my life in South America, my interests. She offers me some more little cakes.

Her extreme politeness and amused kindness make me understand that for her too I am a foreigner; what could I possibly understand of Macumba?

She asks about my past and about the country where I live. For her France evokes, above all else, luxury perfume. She asks whether there is a beach near my house. "No?" She looks at me with pity. "Nevertheless, I have the impression that you were born near the sea." I tell her that I was born in Tunisia, on the Mediterranean coast, and that I only later emigrated to Europe. She doesn't know where Tunisia is. I tell her that it is a small country in North Africa.

"In Africa? You were born in Africa?" She looks at me

incredulously. I am as amazed as she is. I explain to her that North Africa is not exactly what she means by Africa. "Africa is Africa!" she declares categorically. "Our gods come from Africa. Our slave ancestors were also from Africa. Africa is the land of life. You were born there . . . you are one of our own, one of our children."

At this point the conversation becomes much less conventional. All her distrust has vanished. Without realizing it, I have given her the best possible letter of introduction. Maria-José now sees me in a different light. She accepts me. From then on she answers all my questions, concealing her annoyance when she finds them too insipid, or leaping to answer those that particularly interest her. Our conversation goes on late into the night. When she begins to feel tired she invites me to return the next day so that we can continue the discussion, and stretches out her hand for me to kiss her goodbye.

"The gods and spirits descend into the bodies of their children. They come from Africa, drawn by the drums and chants, by the dances of their children and the drawings that we trace in the dirt. They come because they need us just as much as we need them. They like the presents we give them, the candles and incense we burn in their honor, our bodies and our prayers. They come because they know that we are ready to receive them."

"Trances are very difficult for us to accept, and even more difficult to understand. What is their function?"

"My son, our gods and spirits are all we have. We have nothing else. No sacred texts, no monuments, no enduring references. That is both our weakness and our strength.

"If we stopped singing and dancing, if we stopped lending

our bodies to the gods so that they can descend to earth, the gods would leave us. They'd forget us and go off to die in Africa. And our religion would disappear.

"But that is also our strength — it's what makes our religion so alive. We pray to living gods, to gods with power, not to empty forms which once existed and which now are cold and weak.

"We know that our gods are alive because we see them all the time incarnate in the bodies of men and women. You saw them last night. They were here among us. We know that our gods are full of energy — if they weren't there could be no trances."

"Could you explain to me just what happens in a trance?"

"Nothing happens — nothing, at least, in the sense in which you mean it. The mediums lend their bodies to the gods in order for them to become incarnate; so that they can be with us, speak to us, answer our questions, give us strength. It's a kind of exchange. We give life to the gods, and they in return agree to help us.

"The gods need support in order to exist. The role of the medium is to provide that support. When the gods arrive here, in Brazil, they take possession of their children's bodies. They mount them as a rider would a horse. And at that moment the head of the medium exists only as a vessel, a simple vase offered to the god. The medium has no will, no memory, no personality. The god enters the medium and makes herself or himself at home. It's the god you see and hear. Once the god is gone the medium can't remember anything that happened during the trance or any of the things the god may have done or said."

"But what does the medium feel during the ecstasy?"

"There are two forms of possession. The first is violent and brutal; it is extremely undesirable. The medium is sent into convulsions, and I am forced to quiet the god. The second and more common form is progressive and much gentler. It begins with an intermediary state, a light, imperceptible trance which doubtless corresponds to the moment when the consciousness begins to blur. At this point mediums often seem to be returning to their childhood. They laugh, skip and speak in *non sequiturs*. This lasts only a few seconds. Then there's a kind of acceleration and the trance actually begins. Sometimes the childlike beginning stage lasts a bit too long, becoming turbulent and disrupting the whole ceremony. The medium bumps into the dancers, pinches them and plays tricks on them. If that happens I have to intervene.

"But whatever the nature of the trance may be, the personality of the medium has nothing to do with it. One minute the medium is herself and the next minute she no longer exists: the god has entered her body. But these moments are easy to tell apart."

"How does the medium feel once the trance is over?"

"She feels good. Very good. And tired, of course, especially if the trance has been active. But she feels good, because her head has been emptied and in a sense regenerated. And above all because the god has left behind a great strength.

"Still, the dances of possession are not performed simply for the benefit of the medium. On the contrary.

"To be a medium implies sacrifices and constraints which are often extremely difficult. Mediums, more than any of us, must obey our laws. Their role is difficult.

"No, the trance benefits the community most of all; how the medium feels is unimportant since she voluntarily offered her body to the gods. The essential thing is that the gods be able to become incarnate. It is a great honor to receive a god. I think that once the trance is over the mediums think only of their luck in having lent their bodies to the gods."

"Does the trance benefit society?"

"The trance is the basis of our survival. When our ancestors were brought to this country as slaves they brought the gods in their bodies. They never gave up the trance, and that's why the gods never abandoned them. We do everything we can — use all our forces and are ready to give everything we have — so that the gods won't leave us."

"What is done to provoke a trance? Last night I saw women drinking liters of cachaça and smoking big cigars. . . . Is it necessary to be drunk and dizzy before a trance can begin?"

"Of course not, my son. You don't want to understand. . . . When they drink and smoke, the daughters of the gods are already no longer themselves. It is the gods who are drinking and smoking. The woman you mentioned is Teresinha. Yesterday she drank four liters of brandy. Normally she wouldn't be able to. But she's the daughter of Exú, and Exú likes to get drunk. He loves strong cachaça and big, black cigars. Teresinha's body has been given to him so that he can satisfy these desires. After the ceremony she was no more drunk than you or I. She herself had drunk nothing — it was her god."

"Why do the mediums sometimes leave the ceremonial hall and return decked out in various disguises?"

"They are not disguises, they are the signs of their gods.

Sometimes a medium will leave the ceremonial hall — we call it our dance hall — and go to one of the small rooms we call the houses of the gods,[1] where she will kneel before an altar, dressed in the clothes or bearing the weapons of the divinity which has possessed her. Actually it is the god who goes to seek familiar clothes and objects. Yesterday you saw Ogum, the warrior god, return among us wearing his blue satin cape, holding his victory helmet and brandishing the sword with which he works — which he uses to fend off attackers.

"Similarly, a medium possessed by Omulú will return with a straw mask over her face, wearing necklaces of shells and holding a mace covered with braided straw. Such a medium is not 'disguised,' but has simply assumed the appearance of the One she incarnates."

"At one point a fairly young woman suddenly doubled over and began to limp, supporting herself on a cane. She had the voice of an old man. . . ."

"Yes, the spirit of a *preto velho*, an old black man, had descended into her." She points to a shelf on which sits a statue of an old black man with a pipe in his mouth and a cane at his side. "There's a preto velho! The pretos velhos are the spirits of old slaves or of blacks who died a long time ago, who were very wise and had a gift for healing, a broad knowledge of things. They return to earth to help us out, to guide us, and give us advice.

"The spirit can come to any medium. It uses the medium's body to come and save us."

"But why the cane, the pipe and the harsh voice?"

"Because it's an old man. The real age of the medium is

[1]See floor plan of terreiro, p.10.

meaningless during the trance. Even if the preto velho possessed a young person she would still limp, still lean on a cane, and still smoke a pipe. When a spirit or a god descends to earth, it does not change. It continues to do everything it likes to do. It drinks if it likes alcohol, smokes if it wants to, and speaks like an old person because it is old. But these things are unimportant. . . ."

"Do you mean that the behavior of the mediums who were in a trance last night was really that of the gods and spirits incarnate in them?"

"That's exactly what I mean. Xangô speaks with pride. Oxalá is wise and majestic. Oxum is coquettish. When they are in a trance the daughters of Oxum often make themselves up and preen before a mirror. Sometimes the gods take up old quarrels. Oxum and Iemanjá will argue, for example. Over jealousy. And I am forced to separate them."

"Then the children of the gods aren't acting at random when they are in a trance. They follow the major lines of the myths."

"It has nothing to do with myths. It has to do with character. The gods, like ourselves, have personalities — ways of acting, good and bad qualities. The children of gods are not movie stars. They do not play a role. They themselves are absent during the trance. You think we know the history of our gods by heart, and that all we do is repeat it here mechanically, as in a play. No! There are no rehearsals, no roles, no lines learned by heart. Our religion, as I said, is alive! If the gods always act consistently it's because they have no reason to change. But the ceremonies vary; I never know in advance what's going to take place. Sometimes very few mediums fall into a trance. And that's a very bad sign. It means that the gods are sulking. Sometimes the trances are violent, sometimes harmonious. Sometimes a god delivers a warning through the mouth of a medium. None of this can be predicted."

"But is the general format of a ceremony always the same in your terreiro?"

"Some things never change, but of course each holiday is dedicated to a particular god or has a specific purpose. For example, our costumes are not always the same. For the Festival of the Caboclos, the spirits of the old Indians of Brazil, we wear feather headdresses. For Exú, however, I wear red and black satin. And along with the changes in costume there are changes in the dance steps and the rhythms of the drummers. There are definite rules, but each dance or *engira* corresponds to a different celebration."

"It seems that clothing is quite important."

"The costume is only the appearance. It is the materialization of a power; it acts upon the wearer. Ogum without his saber or mirror is not really Ogum. The gods are incomplete without their attributes. The more exactly the formal details are respected — clothing, necklaces, headdresses, accessories — the more powerful the god becomes."

"But how can these objects give strength to the gods?"

"They don't give strength to the gods; they give strength to the incarnations of the gods, to their materialization which acts here on earth. They make this materialization much more effective. Of course alone they don't have much meaning. A ceremonial object outside the ceremony is empty; it has no value. But when it is used by an incarnate god at the proper moment in a dance, for example, it regains its power — it is an indispensable part of the ceremony. You see, a ceremony is perfect only when all the possibilities of the gods have been utilized to the maximum. To give Xangô his ax, Ogum his saber or Omulú her straw clothing is to give them the tools that will let them use their capabilities to the full."

"What is your role during the ceremony?"

"You think I'm the stage director, don't you? That I direct the mediums?"

"At times I've seen you interrupt or stimulate a trance at will."

"I am there to make sure our gods help everyone. I do whatever I can to control the trances so that they are neither dangerous nor ineffective. Sometimes the gods are unaware of their own strength. They forget that their 'horses' can become exhausted. So I calm them down. If they react too violently to a song I soothe them. . . .

"Sometimes, and this has happened recently, an uninitiated person will enter a trance. This person is not ready to receive a god. The god, in this case a Santo Bruto or 'untamed Saint,' has no right over the person, so I ask him to be patient, to wait until his child is initiated to possess her. I console him with prayers and by changing the rhythms of the drums. I call for different songs until he finally goes away.

"You see, the gods and spirits are not that different from you and me. They follow their own natures and obey their own desires. They can be influenced just like people — by ruses, flattery, reason, prayer or material offerings."

"Do you yourself ever go into a trance?"

"[After a sigh] I am a very attentive Mother. If I went into a trance, who would watch over the faithful? Some Mothers of the Gods can't resist the call of the drums. But I personally believe that my role forbids me to enter a trance. Before running the terreiro I, like all initiates, was possessed by my god. I too have known the ecstasy, my son; I too have known it. . . ."

"Are you saying, then, that for a trance to be useful it should not become too violent?"

"That's not what I meant to say. The trance should be harmonious. And that does not necessarily exclude violence. It's in the nature of the possession of certain gods to be brutal. Take Ogum, for example. Ogum is a warrior god. If he decides to be terrible one evening, I don't do anything to stop him. Because it's in his nature to be terrible. On the other hand, if one of the faithful shows a lack of respect for our laws, I can punish that person by leading him or her into a violent crisis. I have made people double over, fall to the floor and bang their heads against a wall. As punishment."

"I don't exactly follow you. You tell me that you can inflict a violent trance as punishment. But what is the punishment, if the medium is not herself, if she remembers nothing when it's all over?"

"It's not that simple. Something in her remembers. Some part of her of which she is unconscious, something deep inside her. Something which exists in all of us at every moment, even during sleep, even when we faint, and which deeply affects our actions. The medium in a trance resembles someone sleeping. Even if we don't remember our dreams we retain an impression of them long after we wake. It's the same thing with a trance.

"The medium who does something bad is unconscious of her action. There is something within her which pushes her to act this way. That 'something' is what I must punish. People often think that blaming, reprimanding or oppressing someone is enough to cure that person's evil tendencies. A murderer is locked in a cell or isolated to prevent him from doing further harm. It's true that protects us from him. But it does absolutely nothing for the criminal himself, because it doesn't go to the root of the problem. When I punish a medium in a trance I bring about a true separation between him or her and the negative forces within."

"Is that 'something' you referred to affected by the entry of the god into the medium's body?"

"Yes. That's what I meant when I said that the trance is energy-giving."

"What does one do to induce a trance? What conditions are necessary for the arrival of the gods?"

"The gods descend when they feel that their children are ready to receive them, that they are capable of offering themselves without resistance. And naturally, when a space has been prepared for their arrival."

"Then a trance can't occur just anywhere?"

"Not a controlled trance. And an uncontrolled trance is quite dangerous. No, first there has to be a sacred space, a terreiro. The terreiro is our temple, an enclosed space where the gods feel at ease. Where they feel at home."

"Are all terreiros located in houses, like your own, or are some of them outdoors or in apartments?"

"In an apartment? That would be impossible, my child! The dancers must be able to touch the ground with their bare feet, to be in direct contact with the earth.

"Of course there are outdoor terreiros. But they are always

enclosed. A simple wooden fence will do, but the space must be clearly marked off, clearly separated from the rest of the world. It is a privileged place. And then there is a whole ritual designed to sanctify it. We decapitate certain animals, offering their blood and flesh to the gods and to the earth, and we bury all sorts of objects in the terreiro floor to give the terreiro its strength.

"The terreiro represents Africa, the source — it is a symbolic, miniature Africa. It is conceived as a place where the gods can find each other. Its floor plan is familiar to them, and they feel safe coming to it. All terreiros, no matter how simple, are built on exactly the same pattern. The terreiro is the land of life, the land of origins, and it is on this site of rediscovered origins that the mediums come to dance."

"You mentioned objects which are buried in the earth. Are they relics? Fetishes?"

"Certain objects are buried, generally near the entrance. Others are displayed. [with an obvious lack of trust] We do not speak of these things. It's not important. . . ."

"I noticed a large vertebra in a niche of your terreiro. Is that one of the special objects?"

"Yes. That was given to us as a present. It comes from the body of a whale that ran aground on one of our beaches."

"What's the connection between the whale and Macumba?"

"The whale is a huge and powerful animal. Nonetheless, like our ancestors, this whale was led across the ocean to die in Brazil. Its bone is an object of power; it gives strength to the terreiro."

"Do the houses of the gods always contain power?"

"Yes. Each terreiro has a special place which we call a *peji,* which is a kind of sanctuary filled with statues of the gods, their attributes, symbols, and so on. Our peji, in this terreiro, is made up of many little rooms which are kept locked, and that's where we store all the possessions of the gods. There's a room for each god."

"Why do you lock the houses of the gods?"

"The peji is a holy place which only the initiated may enter after being ritually cleansed in an herbal bath; and then only if their bodies are in a state of purity. A woman who has her period or anyone who has just had sexual relations is not allowed to enter."

"What's in the houses of the gods?"

"That depends on the god. There are of course the god's accessories — necklaces, weapons, emblems . . . and often there are offerings — food placed on earthenware platters, sacrificed animals, statues, holy images, magical diagrams or herbs. But all of this centers around particular objects of special power which contain great spiritual force. These are called *axés*.

"The axés are the strength of the terreiro. They may be a stone, a piece of iron, or any other object which the god has 'imprinted' in some way and which has come to represent him or her. The axés play an important part in the initiation ceremonies, since by touching them the mediums 'make their heads' — they absorb the spiritual forces that help prepare the way for possession. The strength of the axés comes from the blood of all the animals we sacrifice to them — we sprinkle the blood over them — and also from the soaked herbs we 'bathe' them in."

"What's the difference between the altar in the ceremonial hall, which contains statues of saints, offerings, and so on, and the houses of the gods?"

"They are two sides of the same force. The altar of the dance hall is meant for the audience — it can be seen and touched by all. The houses of the gods are reserved for the initiated. The houses of the gods are the secret part of the terreiro. The place of the mystery. . . . But we do not discuss these things. . . ."

"Do the magic chalk diagrams you draw on the dance floor during the ceremony also have power?"

"Those drawings, the *pontos riscados*, have a very precise function. They are there to complete the effect of the songs — *pontos cantados* or simply *pontos de Macumba*. They help summon the gods. There are hundreds of them. Each one represents a god, a spirit, or a particular aspect of a god or spirit. They are graphic prayers. The symbols we use in them are the language of the gods. We often place a lighted candle in their center so that the gods can see them from a distance.

"The pontos riscados are made with white or colored sticks of chalk which we call *pembas*. I remember that when I was young the pembas were made from African chalk which had been imported at great expense and which produced near-perfect drawings. But today we use Brazilian chalk."

She takes a white pemba from a small bag. It is a piece of chalk the size of a cigarette pack, a long oval shape.

"The pemba is one of the essential elements of our religion. It is not used only for drawing pontos. Sometimes it's used to 'close a body' — *fechar um corpo*; that is, to extract from someone all the evil influences and forces which might otherwise destroy that person, and to seal the body against them."

"How does that work?"

"Using the appropriate pemba, I draw on the person's face

and body a series of lines which intersect at certain points, closing off the places where evil spirits could enter. But only a Mother of the Gods or a medium in a trance knows the exact way to do this."

"Why a medium in a trance?"

"But I've already told you, my child. A medium in a trance is no longer herself; it is the god which has possessed her who acts *through* her."

"Does each ponto riscado have a special meaning, or are they simply magic symbols which aid in summoning the gods?"

"Each one has an exact meaning — they can be read like a text. They are each related to a god or to an aspect of a god, or even to a group of gods. Each terreiro knows its own pontos riscados, but the symbols never change. For example, the sword is associated with Ogum, the arrow with Oxossi, the ax with Xangô, the trident with Exú. The same thing with the color: green is for curing the sick, blue for dances, and so forth."

"Are there also songs for each god?"

"There are innumerable prayers. Each terreiro knows its own. Each one is addressed to a particular god or spirit. Some of them contain African words. Others are completely in 'the language' — in African, generally Yoruba. But the rhythm is more important than the meaning of the words. Our gods respond to rhythm above all else. When the rhythm changes their behavior shifts accordingly.

"The drums intercede on our behalf. They are our most convincing voice. Our instruments are not ordinary, everyday drums. We consider them living beings."

"What distinguishes them from ordinary instruments?"

"They have been 'nourished' by the sacred strength of the

axés. Each drum is regularly sprinkled with the blood of a two-legged animal. In our offerings we distinguish between two- and four-legged animals. For each drum we decapitate a chicken, which is two-legged. Its blood runs down the body of the drum. The drum also 'eats' a candle, palm oil, honey, and chicken which has been prepared and cooked a special way. These offerings stay beside the drum for a whole night so that it fully absorbs their strength. The candle burns itself out in front of the drum.

"Then the drum is baptized with the holy water from a church, in the presence of its godmothers and godfathers. It is given a name.

"We never lend our instruments. They belong to the terreiro. If they came in contact with impurity they would lose their strength and would no longer have the power to make the gods descend. Their voices would be out of tune and the gods would remain deaf to our call. Women who have their period also throw the drums off key."

"I noticed three drums of different sizes."

"Yes. The largest one is the *rum*, the middle one is the *rumpi*, and the smallest is the *lé*. Their sounds have the power to unite all those who hear them in one harmonious vibration. But not just anyone can play them. Only the *ogãs*, skilled musicians initiated for this purpose, know how to make them talk.

"Just as there are chants and drawings for each god, each god also has its favorite rhythms. Oxalá answers to the *Bravun*, Xangô to the *Alujá*, Oxossi to the *Aguerê*. . . . Certain rhythms are tapped with the fingers, others played on sticks. . . ."

"At one point I noticed a kind of double metal bell which you hit with an iron stick."

"That instrument is called an *agogô*. I use it only as a last resort, to make a recalcitrant god descend. No god can resist the call of the agogô!"

"I also noticed that at one point the drums stopped and the rhythm was maintained through the end of the ceremony simply by the clapping of hands. What was the meaning of the change?"

"It was very late, my child." She laughs. "Our drums make a lot of noise and keep the neighbors up. I don't have the right to disturb people's sleep, so we keep the beat in a more discreet way. It's not very significant. By that time of night the gods have already heard our call. And the songs continue."

"What are these songs? I suppose they are a central element in summoning the gods?"

"No, my son. The most important thing is the rhythm. You see, it comes from Africa."

"But you yourself said that very few of them are 'in the language,' that most of the words are in Portuguese. . . ."

"The words don't matter. Our songs come directly from Africa. I'm not saying that they haven't changed since slavery. I'm saying that they all spring from a single African source. It's possible there may be some Indian influence, but it's very slight.

"Our African ancestors were stripped of everything by their masters. Stripped of all material things. But the rhythms of their native land were deeply rooted in their minds. Even when they were forbidden, they survived in memory. And when they were converted the slaves sang the Christian prayers to the only melodies they knew. That was the only way they had of keeping their identity. The only tie to their true essence, the Land of Life, the Africa of their birth. I think all

Brazilian popular music, even the samba and the bossa nova, comes from our mother Africa."

"How do you determine the order in which the gods are summoned?"

"There is a fixed order for calling them. Each terreiro has its own. Sometimes certain gods do not honor it and arrive when no one is expecting them; then I am forced to send them away. They have to follow the order. It's a question of etiquette. The ceremony always starts with a call to a god who is able to 'open the path.' Exú is the guardian of thresholds and master of doors; he is the first to be named. If he weren't first he'd get angry and disrupt the ceremony, preventing it from going on. Ogum is also an opener of the path. He is called next. Then we let the youngest, most fiery gods descend, since they respond most quickly to our calls. They are eager for life and impatient to enjoy our gifts and bodies. They are bubbling with energy and fall upon us as if they were starving.

"We sing at least three prayers to each god. Never fewer. That gives them the time to hear us."

"You consider the words unimportant?"

"Generally speaking the prayers are simple words of praise. Sometimes the songs recount the history of the gods or the most important incidents of their lives. We strive above all to attract them by showing them how well we know them and love them, and how anxiously we await their arrival.

"For example, in honor of Oxum we sing:

> My Mother Oxum,
> queen of lakes and rivers!
> My Mother Oxum,
> hear our words,

bring us happiness!
My Mother Oxum,
when you leave
we fill with grief.

"And for Omulú:

Here comes old Omulú,
slowly drawing near,
here comes old Omulú,
limping along!

"The gods recognize themselves in these words and reply to our message. But they also recognize themselves in our dances. Each song corresponds to a particular dance."

"Yet the dances seemed quite similar to me. I had the impression that only a trance could disturb them."

"A trance does not disturb a dance! It gives it its true dimension. The details that differentiate one dance from another are minute: they are the gestured accompaniment to the songs. When the god appears the dance is no longer a simple call. The moment a trance begins the dance becomes what it should always be: the gait and behavior of that particular god. It is not disturbed — it is magnified.

"Each god dances in his or her own special way. Look! Oxossi the hunter always has one foot forward, Iemanjá and Oxum spin around making signs with their hands, and Ogum the warrior seems always to be fighting invisible enemies!

"Yes, our gods arrive dancing. And the body of the medium should move to the rhythm of her master. The medium lets herself be tamed like a horse. And when she surrenders and becomes an 'easy mount' we know that the god is at home in her. At that point we give the gods their symbols. Ogum receives his sword, Oxossi his bow, Oxum her fan. And the gods begin to do the things which are familiar to them."

"Is it at that point that the faithful can seek the gods' assistance?"

"Yes, at that moment the gods are ready to respond. They have received what they wanted. They have been 'fed.' Now they can be questioned. They can be asked all kinds of things — about health, about financial or romantic problems. . . . The gods give their advice, prescribe treatments, demand offerings. If their opinions are followed to the letter, the results are almost immediate. We no longer keep track of our successes. Those whose wishes were fulfilled because of us often return to see us and give gifts to the center."

"Do these gifts alone support the terreiro? Don't you charge anything for the service you provide?"

"Terreiros live on donations. Each member gives what he or she can, according to their means. But we never ask for anything. If we asked for money we would lose all our powers. The gods and spirits would run away from us. The few terreiros which *have* tried to make money fell apart very quickly.

"The mediums who lend their bodies to the gods do not receive a salary either. They all have regular jobs during the day. They join us when they can, because they want to. They receive the gift of offering their bodies, which is too precious a gift to be wasted. They all know this and are conscious of their mission. They come here of their own free will to help their neighbors."

"Then not just anyone can be a medium?"

"That's right. You can't choose to become one. You either

are one or you aren't. Certain gifts can be developed, but you have to have the basic disposition. One of my jobs is to recognize the future medium in a visitor. But generally the gods themselves choose their mounts. They appear in sleep, or savagely mount those they have chosen. Sometimes a medium in a trance will grab a member of the audience and carry him or her around the room on her shoulders, repeating the ritual greeting. That is how the gods announce their desire to ride a person in whom they have detected a vocation!"

"Before attending a ceremony, I thought that all the participants went into trances. But now I see that only the initiates are possessed."

"Yes, I know that outsiders think all we do is scream like animals and roll on the ground. . . .

"But the trance is not an end in itself. Only the initiated can experience it, people who have a natural gift as mediums, who have been prepared for the experience.

"These people are initiated by us, right here. An initiation is a kind of pact with a god, the god who is the 'master of the head' — *dono da cabeça* — of the medium. The initiates are always possessed by the same god, the exclusive master of their head. They go into a trance when the god responds to their call."

"What does one do to get initiated?"

"Well, let's suppose that a young woman — you've probably noticed that the majority of our followers are female — wants to be initiated, either because she feels she has a gift or because a god has chosen her. She comes to see me and tells me of her decision. First I must ask the *buzios*, the cowrie shells, whether there is anything that might go against her wish. If the answer is negative, the young woman prepares her trousseau and comes to live in the terreiro.

"She takes off her old clothes and receives her new ones. At dawn she is washed with sacred herbs and her head is rubbed with pure water — water from a waterfall or fountain. This marks the end of her secular life. From that point on she must speak as little as possible, and only with initiates of the terreiro. She forgets her parents and friends and devotes herself entirely to her new status. During the final days of the initiation she can express herself only in sign language. She claps her hands three times if she wants someone's attention.

"The initiation lasts several months. Initiation is not the revelation of obscure secrets during the course of a terrifying ritual, as people sometimes think. It simply tries to develop the 'mediumness' of the novice's 'other personality,' the personality of her god. It begins with the discovery of the identity of her master of the head. Here too the cowrie shells, our oracle, play an important part.

"When I know for sure which god controls the novice's head I bind the child to her god with a pact. The novice begins to wear the god's necklace. Xangô's necklace is made of red and white glass beads; Iemanjá's of transparent ones; Ogum's is yellow; Oxossi's green. . . .

"This necklace or *kelê* is a sign of submission to the god. It is regularly touched to the god's axé, rubbed with herbs and soaked in the blood of sacrificial animals.

"The head of the aspiring initiate is still weak. It is not ready to receive its god. My first task is to strengthen it. I feed it, fortify it, fill it with sacred forces.

"I can't reveal too many of our secrets to you. Some of them are too holy to be exposed to the light of day. But I will point out to you the most important parts of the operation.

"All of our ceremonies begin with bloody sacrifices. You see, blood is the mainstay of the energy that constitutes the strength of things and living beings. After the reciting of formulas and prayers asking for the blessing of the gods, we decapitate a rooster by pulling off its head and let its blood rush over the face and body of the novice. We also keep a piece of the animal and place it in front of an effigy of the god who is the master of the head of the future initiate. This first communion in blood has a double purpose: to bind the child to her god and to nourish her head. The blood coagulates and dries on her body and she remains awake, without moving, for a whole night, so that the 'contact' is firmly established.

"The next stage is the permanent entry of the god into the head of the child. Throughout this period the novice is confined to a small room in the heart of the terreiro; this room is known as a *camarinha*. She is cut off from her family and from the outside world. She must be pure and abstain from sexual relations. She is regularly 'washed' in a bath of herbs which has been consecrated to her god. It is like a progressive death, and at the end she will be reborn purified, different, sanctified. She learns our songs, our laws and our customs. She discovers all the responsibilities of the position she is about to assume. She sews, by hand, the clothing for her initiation.

"The novice can't go outside into the street because her head must not receive rain, sun or even wind. She observes the dietary taboos, which vary according to who is master of her head. On some days of the week she has to remain in bed; on others she has to stay on her feet.

"The blood baths continue. First two-legged animals, then

four-legged ones are slaughtered. The former personality of the novice is destroyed or, more accurately, erased, and a new one is created in its place. Little by little she becomes a *yaõ*, a 'bride' of her god.

"When I'm convinced that the god and the yaõ are finally ready to become united, the novice experiences her first controlled trance. The drums begin to beat. Barefoot and dressed all in white, alone in the center of the ceremonial hall, the yaõ receives her god. The trance should not come on too suddenly. She turns slowly in place and the god possesses her 'gently.' Then we all applaud and set off firecrackers outside the terreiro to express our joy on seeing a god discover a new body to descend to earth in.

"I make sure that the trance is authentic — that she hasn't just been acting — by passing a lighted candle over the naked arms of the new yaõ."

"Do you mean to say that she consciously lets herself be burned?"

"There is no burn. Not if the trance is real. The flame licks the skin without causing the slightest pain or mark. If it did it would mean that the novice, ashamed of not being able to be possessed, was only pretending. But in a genuine trance the yaõ feels nothing."

"Then is the young woman ready to take part in all the ceremonies?"

"Not yet, my child, not yet. . . . She must still receive a name and be 'confirmed'; she still has to reenter the outside world.

"The medium is the son or daughter of a god. But each 'incarnated' god has a kind of surname, the *dijina*, which is how he or she prefers to be known, and which corresponds to a particular aspect of his or her personality. After several years of work, the medium will receive a new dijina which corresponds to the position she has reached in the hierarchy of our cult. The name of a god who has been 'linked to a head' — *já na cabeça* — for many years is not the same as that of a god who has only recently acquired a body."

"How do you determine what the names should be?"

"But I'm not the one who determines the names — it's the gods themselves! I said that it is *their* choice, *their* preference. When the novice goes into a trance the god appears and gives the dijina. Oxum, for example, may be called Epondá, Apará or Eubambá. . . .

"Besides the naming ceremony there are ceremonies for making offerings. Perhaps the most important of these is the Ceremony of Plants. In some ways it corresponds to the 'resurrection' of the novice. On that day the yaõ leaves the 'little room' carrying a jar of her axé's water on her back. We are supposed to help her. She is in a daze and walks hesitatingly, like someone just relearning how to walk. Supported by the sons and daughters of the gods of the terreiro, she is presented to me once again. She makes the ritual greeting, greeting first me, then the altar, the gods, and all the assembled initiates. After walking around the whole terreiro and dancing and making offerings to the dead and to the spirits, she is led outside and washed with the water of her axé. It is then that she publicly reveals her initiation name, her dijina.

"Then she is ready to rejoin the outside world. She returns to her family. All that remains to be done is for her to be blessed in a Catholic church on the first Friday of the next month."

"In a church?"

"Yes, in a Catholic church, with holy water. And then the most important thing, as I said, is for her to rediscover the outside world, to readjust herself to a normal life. Don't forget that she hasn't been outside the terreiro even once during the whole initiation period. So she has to be bought back by her family."

"What do you mean, bought back?"

"My child, an initiation costs a lot of money. We have to sacrifice many animals and feed the young woman. The terreiro alone can't be expected to shoulder the financial burden. So there is a huge party, at which the young woman must be bought back by her family. It's like an auction, except that the price is set in advance and simply covers our expenses — the price of an initiation can run as high as eight or nine hundred dollars. Then the young woman is free to return home. I gave you the example of a young woman, but of course the initiation of a man follows a similar pattern."

"Can the initiate lead a normal life — marry and have children, for example?"

"Of course. All initiates choose the private life they wish to lead. Their only obligations concern our religion, and only minimally affect their daily lives."

"What are these obligations?"

"Faith and charity direct the thoughts and actions of the children of the gods. They fulfill their obligations with faith and charity. The obligations are two-fold: toward the terreiro, and toward their god.

"The children of the gods are expected to participate in all the ceremonies, dances and festivities of the terreiro. They owe respect to their Mae de Santo and to those of their sisters and brothers in Oxalá who are older than they — those who were initiated before them, whether or not they are chronologically older. They help me and my assistant in the preparation of the ceremonies. They see to the upkeep and appearance of the terreiro. They are required to help anyone who seeks their services. Under no circumstances are they to ask for or accept any payment for the help they provide."

"At what age can a person be initiated?"

"Age is unimportant. There are children who show their vocation as mediums at a very early age. On the other hand, for others the need for initiation does not show up until much later in life. Of course, the earlier you are initiated the greater your chance of acquiring a complete knowledge of our religion. Don't forget, this can come only through experience. Time and time alone will let you master all the powers."

"Can anybody be initiated? I noticed many whites among your mediums."

"The color of a person's skin is unimportant. We're no longer at the point when only blacks and mulattos were initiated. Our followers come from every sector of Brazilian society. We have no social or racial prejudice. But not everyone can experience the trance. As I was telling you, you have to have a certain disposition — the ability to surrender totally to your god."

"Can a foreigner be initiated?"

"I don't know; that depends on the individual. But why not? Though — I don't know — foreigners have a lot of obstacles in their heads, prejudices which block them and keep them from letting go completely, from becoming malleable, from emptying their heads enough to let a god inside.

"I once knew a Dutch woman who was a medium in a terreiro. She had attended several ceremonies out of curiosity and each time she had been savagely mounted by her god. At first she didn't want to recognize what was happening. She would say, 'I don't understand this. It's like a superior force which invades me and against which I am powerless.' Finally she realized that she was predestined to it, and that she would be more at peace with herself, more fulfilled, if she was initiated. She was a daughter of Xangô and became a very good medium. She had had no previous intimation of her gifts. It was the contact with the terreiro, with the holy universe of Macumba, that revealed them to her.

"But in general foreigners are too limited by their education. They are frightened of our dances and our sacrifices. And then they are afraid of being 'lowered' by accepting what they consider our silly superstitions. They see the evidence with their eyes and deny it with their minds. Their bodies say yes but their spirits say no. They hold out obstinately behind the idea that these things have no place in a civilized world."

"Maria-José, do you think that I could experience a trance?"

She laughs. "I really don't think so, my child. I think you could understand us. You were born in Africa — in that you have a great advantage. But you lack the gift. . . . I'm afraid the honor of the trance would be denied you."

"If you had sensed that I had the powers of a medium, would you have advised me to become one?"

"Without a doubt. But I wouldn't have forced you. It's a serious decision, one which would be nobody's concern but your own. But certainly I would have advised you to become one, yes. . . .

"As I said before, the gift is too rare to be wasted. We're not lacking mediums, and there are many men and women who would like to join our ranks. But there will never be enough. And besides, I think it's dangerous for a person to refuse the chance which has been offered."

"How could that be dangerous?"

"Some of them need the trance. Trances are desirable for anyone who has more energy than he or she can handle. People are like furnaces. If they are under-nourished they are cold and useless; they become leeches, parasites who feed on other people's energy. But if instead they are too full of magic forces, they can explode. Macumba takes the energy circulating in the world and channels it, redistributes it according to need. It's a safety valve for some people, a source of energy for others.

"I can't tell if you're following me. The world is full of great floods of energy that circulate and swirl in the greatest chaos imaginable. This energy is not used as it could be. It is not controlled. Left in its raw state, it can drag us along on its path of destruction like a tornado which sucks up everything in sight. Our work in the terreiro strives to capture this energy, to tame it and use it.

"People criticize the violence of our dances. But we don't create that violence. It exists. It's already there, and it would quickly become very dangerous if it could not be expressed, if it weren't freed. Those who deny its existence simply push it under, and deep inside them a terrible force builds up which sooner or later will have to explode. We accept the destructive side of the vital energy within us: it is a force that has to be recognized.

"To refuse this energy would be to deny a part of ourselves.

I knew a man who stubbornly refused to join us. I sensed a powerful medium within him, and repeatedly invited him to be initiated. He respected us, but could not accept the idea of 'marrying' our gods. I suppose he had too high an opinion of himself. He was the victim of his own obstinacy."

"What do you mean?"

"He was possessed by very powerful forces. I had warned him. One day the pressure got too strong and he exploded."

"What do you mean?"

"He was a good and honest man, but very limited and very closed. Everyone agreed he wouldn't hurt a fly. But that was just the mask he wore. I told him he was hurting himself. Well, he killed a man. With a knife. And he was arrested."

"Could Macumba have prevented that murder?"

"Not only would it have prevented it, but the excess strength of the man would have been put to good use. He would have learned how to direct it. He would have nourished the gods."

"Maria-José, not all the faithful who come to you are initiates. How does Macumba work for them?"

"Macumba is a system, a whole, and it functions like a well-oiled machine. It is not even necessary to believe in it to benefit from it — or to be harmed by it.

"From the moment the machine is set in motion the results are inevitable. If a sorcerer puts a hex on you, it doesn't do you any good to laugh: you will still be the victim. The majority of our followers do what the gods tell them to without understanding. But the gods don't need human understanding. You see, for example, I don't know anything about electricity. I could never explain to you how it works. And yet I know that when I push that button I will light the lamp on the table, that when I flick that switch the radio will begin to play. Isn't that what counts? Macumba can't be explained, all you can do is see its effect. It's practiced not with the mind but with the body. What you feel is more important than what you think. If people only learned to follow their intuition they would behave a lot better than they do."

"How would you define your religion?"

"Macumba is like a central axis, a center — human action orders itself harmoniously around it."

"I'd like to know more about it. What can I do to get closer?"

"First of all you have to know who is master of your head, which god presides over your destiny. Come see me again some afternoon around four o'clock. I'll consult the oracle for you and we'll find out whose child you are."

"I'd like to ask you one last question. When all the advice-seekers have left and you want to end a trance, what do you do to bring the mediums back to their normal state?"

"It's very simple. We send the gods out of the mediums' bodies; we chase them from the terreiro. The trance shouldn't last too long. If it did, the children of the gods could lose their minds. So we ask the gods to leave by singing the psalms which correspond to each of them, this time in reverse order. Sometimes a god or spirit refuses to leave the body of his or her child. In such a case I recite some special prayers and blow pipe smoke in the medium's face. If none of that works I force the medium to drink a glass of cold water. The gods fear cold water more than anything, my son."

THE MASTER OF THE HEAD

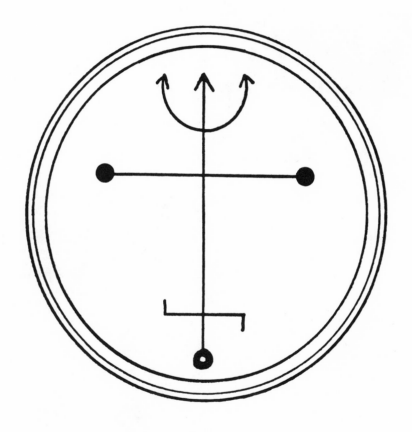

Graphic Invocation of Exú:
Exú Tranca Ruas

A young male yaõ, a prospective medium, on the day of his initiation.

The yaõ leaves the inner sanctuary of the terreiro - the peji - carrying on his shoulder a jar containing water in which his axé or "spiritual object" has been bathed.

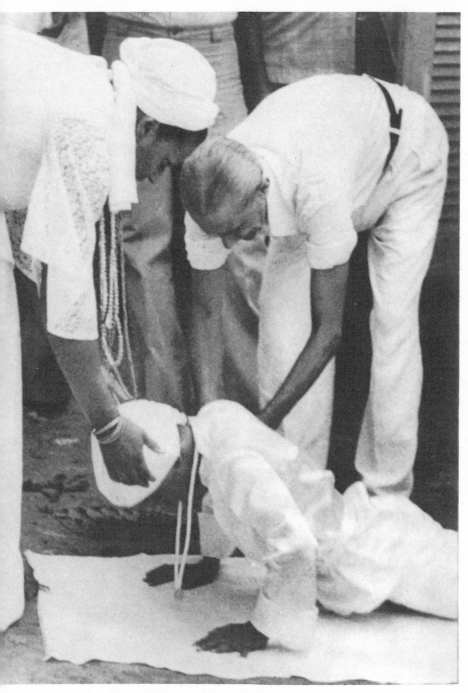

The yaõ is presented to the Mother of the Gods.

Inside a peji or inner sanctuary: the house of Omulú, the god of diseases, cemeteries, and the poor.

Charity collections in the name of Omulú, "Doctor of the Poor."

Statue of a preto velho, an old black woman, inside a "house of Umbanda."

Statues of a caboclo or Indian spirit, and two pretos velhos.

The Festival of Iemanjá, held on the beach, December 31.

The Mother of the Gods of a terreiro (right), with her "little Mother" (left).

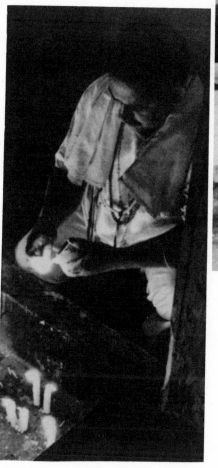

Candle offerings in front of the "cross of faith" and the house of egums, the spirits of the dead.

Street vendor of candles for the spirits in front of a church in Rio de Janeiro on Monday, the Day of the Spirits.

The blessing of a child.

Blessing of children during a ceremony for the Ibejis, the children spirits.

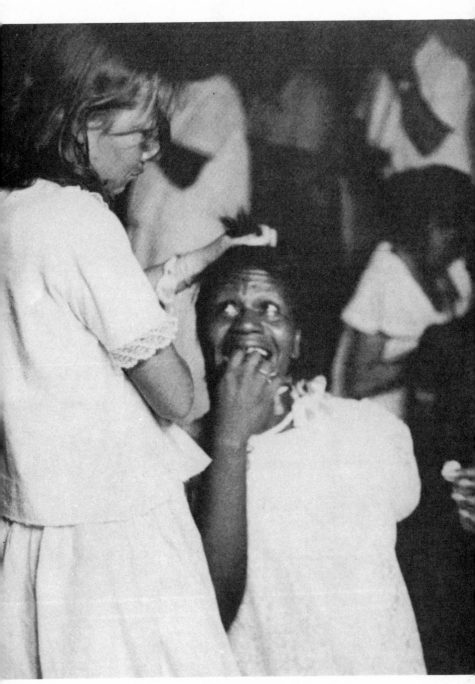

A medium seized by an "infantile" trance, called an eré.

THE MASTER OF THE HEAD

> *Forces of Bahia*
> *Black Forces,*
> *Forces of Africa . . .*

IT is four o'clock in the afternoon. I knock at the terreiro door. A window opens. Someone leans out, recognizes me and comes around to let me in. I explain that I have an appointment with the Mother for a consultation. I'm told she's taking her siesta, but that she won't be long. I should sit down and wait.

By day the ceremonial room resembles the meeting room of a town hall in the provinces. The miniature paper flags on the ceiling give it a festive air. The benches are arranged along the walls. A broom leans against a chair. Fresh flowers have been put in all the vases.

Half an hour goes by. The Mother is still sleeping. The woman who let me into the terreiro asks if I would like a drink. She disappears behind a curtain and returns with a glass of ice-cold water.

Someone knocks at the front door. Another visitor, a woman with a little girl about three or four years old, is ushered in. The same explanations are exchanged. The woman and her child sit down on a bench. The little girl stretches out and falls asleep.

A small garden with palm trees and mangoes can be seen through a window. The afternoon is marvelously calm. Outside, children play in the street. From time to time the sound of a car is heard in the distance.

At about six-thirty I hear busy footsteps in the corridor. The terreiro is coming to life. Maria-José is awake. An old woman leads me to the Mother's room. Maria-José is seated on her bed. She welcomes me. A young woman is knitting in a corner. The long, narrow room is cluttered with objects. In front of the window there is an enormous television on a table covered with a red plastic cloth. White flowers are scattered here and there throughout the room. In one corner there is a huge electric fan. A rosary of large wooden beads hangs from a wall. There is a shelf filled with glass flasks and colored boxes. A sewing machine can be seen behind the door.

The Mother asks that a table be placed in front of her. She covers it with an embroidered white cloth. I sit opposite her, facing her across the table. The young woman continues to knit without raising her eyes. The Mother chases a fly with one hand, complaining about the overpowering heat and hoping that rain will refresh the atmosphere.

As she speaks, chatting about this and that, she takes a fine chrome chain and arranges it before her on the table in the shape of a *U*, the open mouth of the *U* directly facing her. Around it in a circle she places some pebbles she has taken from a small cloth bag. Then she opens a bottle and takes out sixteen white cowrie shells, each with the upper part carefully removed.

Suddenly she stops talking and, without the least transition, her eyes half closed, face raised to the sky, begins to pray in a voice so low that I cannot make out the words.

She pounds her fist angrily on the table several times, each time murmuring a name. She repeats the name insistently and pounds the table again. She collects the cowrie shells in her right hand, and holds them in front of my forehead. Then she shakes the shells in both hands and tosses them into the open space inside the *U*-shape of the chain. She opens her eyes and looks at them, continuing to mumble various formulas. Some of the shells have fallen face up, others face down. She sorts them according to how they have fallen, and counts them on her fingers. She picks up four of them and throws them again. This operation is repeated several times. Then she looks at me and says, "May the Lord of Heaven be with you, my son!" She proceeds to ask me various questions — about my personal relationships, my work, and where I live. She draws a psychological portrait of me which is exact in every respect.

She throws the shells again. According to the way they fall they form a "word," a figure which she interprets. It's similar to geomancy. She asks a question, throws the shells and gives her interpretation, then repeats the whole procedure to verify what she has found.

Finally, she determines that Oxalá is definitely my father. "The oldest of the Oxalás," she explains. "I thought so from the start, but I wanted the shells to confirm my intuition."

"My child, so long as your god is with you, you have nothing to fear. But you must be careful never to offend him." She gives me a series of do's and don'ts, describing in detail the precautions I must take "so that a good relationship persists" between my god and me.

"Oxum, the goddess of fresh water, is also with you. She follows and watches you. From time to time, remember to offer her presents."

The followers of Umbanda generally wear the necklace of their god. She gives me the name of a House of Umbanda[1] where I can buy one. "Come back and see me tomorrow in the afternoon. I'll fix your necklace and we can talk again." And to let me know that our session is over she holds out her hand for me to kiss.

"This necklace links you to your god. It shows that you belong to Oxalá. You wanted to know who was the master of your head. From now on you are linked to him. The beads of the necklace are white, because white is the color of your god. This necklace was washed in our terreiro, which links you to us also. Wear it and go in peace, my son, with Oxalá's protection."

---

[1] Shop which sells the religious articles used in Macumba. Statues of saints, herbs, soaps, bathsalts dedicated to the gods, candles, talismans and other symbols are all thrown together in a jumble. There is at least one in every section of every town and city in Brazil.

"What do you mean when you say it's been 'washed'?"

"My child, ordinary glass beads have no special power. Their strength comes from having been in contact with your god. By itself this necklace is nothing. But we soaked it in a bath of herbs, and that's what's given it its value.

"Each god has his or her own plants. We cut the leaves and soak them in water. The necklace is immersed in the liquid which results. It is washed — that is to say, transformed from a profane object to a sacred one, an object full of energy.

"This necklace is of value only to you. It's useless to anyone else. If you lost it and someone found it and put it on, it would once again become an ordinary glass bead necklace."

"What do you mean by 'belonging to a god'?"

"People usually think they are alone in life. But we are never alone. Never. Not for a minute. We are born under the sign of a god, and this god is the master of our head. He or she accompanies us till the day we die. Our god is our guide and our protector."

"Is the master of the head a kind of guardian angel?"

"It's much more than that. When you were born you inherited the qualities of your god — and also his or her weaknesses, of course. You might say that your god is your deepest nature. Don't forget. You are his son. His spiritual son. That's why knowing him is a way of knowing yourself better.

"He is also your ally, since he numbers you among his own. You can call on him if you are in need. He is ready to help you. He is your strength and your support.

"When you wear his necklace you are linked to him by a covenant. In a sense the two of you have signed a contract. If you fulfill your obligations toward him, he will be your strength."

"What are these obligations?"

"Each god has particular tastes. You must be aware of them. Like everyone else, the gods love presents. Oxalá is fond of white candles. From time to time light a candle for him and let it burn itself out. Offer him a glass of clear water and white flowers. He likes certain dishes: rice cooked with either milk or water, but without salt, millet, new corn, and never any spices. These foods will please him. Leave them overnight in front of his effigy, or simply place them on a clean white cloth. He will eat them. He will like these presents.

"It's said that one day Oxalá refused to give a man salt. Now he is being punished and is allowed no salt with his meals. But above all, never do anything that might displease him. Oxalá is not too demanding of his children. He doesn't ask for much. But you must be careful not to cross him. He'll turn against you if you do. And if that happens you'll have to make a special sacrifice to him."

"What kind of behavior would lead a god to turn against one of his children?"

"The gods don't like to be deprived of the source of their strength. One of our faithful was a daughter of Iemanjá. Daughters of Iemanjá are supposed to wear their hair long. This is good for them. But this woman wanted to be fashionable, so she cut her hair. The goddess abandoned her and persecuted her until the day I advised her to sacrifice a pigeon. Without her hair she had lost her strength; she was in continuous pain, complaining of headaches and dreaming that she was drowning — Iemanjá is goddess of the sea. She recovered only after she had killed the pigeon.

"You see, your god knows what is good for you and what is

good for him. His tastes are the tastes of your own deep nature, even though you yourself may be unaware of them.

"Oxalá, for example, likes white; so white is your special color. He likes white food, the sky and the mountains. He is afraid of fire and distrusts violence. He is distant, and that can sometimes keep him from understanding and lead him into solitude. He is fundamentally generous. He hates to be pestered. He is active without being quick. He's more at ease in time, over a span of time, than in the moment. . . . The list is endless. You'll get to know him little by little. And you'll see that whatever is pleasing to your god is equally good for yourself.

"Certain places, certain days of the week and certain times of day are favorable to you. Others, however, are dangerous. You must be careful never to find yourself in a position of weakness. This law should govern your life."

"Is there a connection between the astrological sign we are born under and the god we are the children of?"

"I don't know much about the stars. I think the two systems resemble each other, but have nothing in common. By that I mean there are no clear parallels between them. Perhaps the stars too permit us to understand ourselves better, but they aren't allies we can count on. The stars follow their own course and affect our destiny. But how can we affect them? Our gods can be cajoled; it's easy to get favors from them. The stars are useful for prediction. But our religion's not as fatalistic as that. We're interested in helping people to help themselves by themselves. Our religion gives the faithful a way to get rid of the negative forces that block and harm them."

"What forces do you mean?"

"When people get involved in a project, whatever it is, and it fails, they complain and say, 'Oh, what bad luck. But it's not my fault. There's nothing I can do about it.' People attribute failure and success to chance. But I don't believe in chance. I believe that luck can be created. I'd say that people find themselves facing negative forces which they don't know how to control.

"We live at the center of a network of active and invisible forces. These forces exist within us and outside us. They push us, stop us, throw us about or allow us to advance, and we go on completely unaware of them. Some of them are positive, some negative. They are everywhere in the world. They are the life of the universe.

"One of the essential values of our religion is that it permits us to act upon this network of forces, to untie the knots which obstruct our life line. It teaches us to store up the positive within us and neutralize the things which oppose us. That's why I said that you create your own luck. We create our luck according to the rules which smooth our way.

"In everything we undertake our god, the one I call the master of our head, is our main ally. All initiations into Macumba begin with the discovery of our god's identity. If we're careful to maintain a good relationship with him, he is the most powerful force within us, and the most creative. Our god is the full range of our possibilities."

"You said I was the son of Oxalá, but that Oxum 'was also with me.' Can one be the child of more than one god?"

"Human beings are complex. All of us contain two opposing or complementary tendencies. Only rarely is a person all of a piece. Oxalá is your major influence. But he's only one part of you. Oxum rules the other side of your being. You were talking about astrology, in which there is also an ascending sign. Don't forget to invoke her in your prayers: she too will come to your aid. But Oxum is more capricious than Oxalá, harder to convince . . . and she also tends to be jealous."

"Is Oxum my guide on all occasions, or does she correspond only to a particular aspect of my personality?"

"You always want to put things in categories!" She sighs. "It's not that simple. The lines of the gods cross, and the meeting of two gods produces a particular conjunction. You aren't seventy percent the son of Oxalá and thirty percent the son of Oxum. That would be completely meaningless, since there is a huge number of additional spirits that influences you which it would be impossible to catalogue. You are simply the son of Oxalá with — in conjunction with — Oxum: *filho de Oxalá com Oxum*. And Oxalá-with-Oxum represents a particular force. It is a whole.

"If, for example, I invoke Omulú-with-Exú, I'm calling on neither of the two but on the power, the entity, created by their conjunction."

"How does the system of divination with shells work?"

"We crack our shells in half, so that when we throw them they have an equal chance of falling face up or face down. One of the sides is male, the other female; one negative, the other positive. Look at this side, it looks like a woman's genitals. Look at this side: it looks like the genitals of a man. These sides symbolize respectively the two aspects of the active energy that moves the universe. Their combinations reveal the gods in all their aspects.

"Before throwing the cowrie shells I ask Exú to be kind

enough to answer all my questions. Certain prayers force him to reveal himself. Exú is not a god of divination. The god of divination is no longer in Brazil; he has returned to Africa."

"What do you mean?"

"Ifa was the god of becoming, and the priest of his cult was known as a Babalaô. That was his name in the language, in Yoruba. The Babalaôs were men of great wisdom. Their knowledge was immense, far superior to our own. When I was young I once met an authentic Babalaô in Salvador.[1] A wise man. He read people's hearts the way you or I would read a book. He had dedicated his life to learning our religion. He spoke the language as well as he spoke Portuguese.

"He worked at home, in a little dark room set aside especially for that purpose. The Mothers of the Gods of many terreiros came to consult him. He answered every question that was put to him without ever making a single mistake. He could tell the exact place and time that were propitious for things. He was a quiet man who spoke little. He measured every word, and none of his gestures was wasted. He led what I would call a perfect life — everything he did, everything that surrounded him and everything he touched was his. He was reflected in everything, and I'm sure that on the day he died he didn't regret a single thing he'd done.

"The Babalaôs didn't use shells. They used the *opele*, the necklace of Ifa. Sometimes the shells lie, for they are an attribute of Exú and Exú is a jokester. But the opele is never wrong.

"To the best of my knowledge there are no more Babalaôs in Brazil. They all went back to Africa, they are dead. The bur-

[1] Capital of the Brazilian state of Bahia.

dens of their role were too great. Nobody can give his life to just that one activity.

"So we Mothers of the Gods ask Exú, the intermediary between gods and human beings, to place us in contact with the gods and so help the well-being of the terreiro."

"But isn't there anyone to take over their job?"

"No. There can't be a woman Babalaô because the cult of Ifa is restricted to men. There are Fathers of Gods who use the title for their own prestige. But they're charlatans. They don't have the right.

"Babalaô means Father of the Mystery in the language. That tells you everything! The Babalaôs held the key to the greatest of all mysteries: Time."

"Why do you consider time the greatest of all mysteries?"

"Because time, my child, is what makes us suffer, and at the same time is what gives things their value. Time is synonymous with life. But it's useless to talk about all that. You can get lost in words."

"Do you mean we shouldn't wonder about these things?"

"It's always good to wonder; but you shouldn't get lost. It's wiser to experience things than to think about them. At least that way you don't get weaker and you don't get tangled up in words."

"That's the second time you've warned me about words."

"My son, the danger of words is that rapidly they become indispensable. They don't always correspond to something. Words are useful only when they refer to things that really exist — otherwise they're just traps for the spirit.

"I'll give you an example. I often receive visits from people who have psychological problems they cannot resolve alone.

They're usually educated people like you. They describe their personal problems and tell me about their anguish. Then I understand that they are locked in prisons of words which they can't escape from. That is, they believe in values that aren't real. I didn't say 'that don't exist'; I'm talking about values which exist only in their minds and not in reality.

"Take a newspaper and open it to any page. You'll find piles of words which are nothing but ideas; they don't refer to anything that has concrete existence. These words have a certain usefulness: they help explain things, they make life easier, they permit us to say all sorts of stupid things about things we don't understand. But the moment we can no longer do without them they turn into traps — prisons of words, of emptiness and anguish. That's why there are some things I'd prefer not to talk about. I don't want to use meaningless words. If you want some good advice, take a good look at your vocabulary, and make sure that no imposters have crept in!"

"What are those shells you use for divination?"

"The set of buzios is for women. Men don't have the right to touch them. The shells I use are from Angola. You can buy them in any market, but to have them speak correctly you have to prepare them — wash them — a special way."

"But there are cowrie shells on every Brazilian beach. Why bring them all the way from Africa?"

"A long time ago the people tried Brazilian ones. But they didn't work. The Brazilian shells aren't holy. They have no power. They don't speak. Only the African cowries answer our questions.

"You must have noticed that before throwing them I used a chain to mark off a space where they were supposed to fall.

That's an 'enchanted' circle. Because, as I said, the gods reveal themselves only in a place that has been prepared for them. They like to be awaited; they like special things to be done for them."

"Do the pebbles you arranged on the table have a special significance?"

"The pebbles are the strength of the earth. Our divination must pass through the earth or it doesn't work. I marked off a space which I sanctified with them. Then I touched your forehead with my hand, and that established a contact between the cowrie shells and you. Because the skull is the seat of the master of the head. That's where it lives. And then I asked your god to reveal himself. But I was sure beforehand that it would be Oxalá."

"How could you be sure before even consulting the oracle?"

"From your way of walking and sitting down. From the shape of your features, thanks to which I could figure out your temperament. In divination intuition is almost as important as knowledge of the 'figures.' All the signs of our god are visible on us. She reveals herself in our tastes, our reactions, our instinctive reflexes — in everything our education, our culture and our social upbringing have not been able to affect. One day a man confessed to me that he experienced a kind of secret joy on stormy days. From that alone I was almost certain that his god was Iansã, goddess of the wind. The wind was his strength. The shells confirmed my intuition."

"How do you read the oracle?"

"When the buzios fall on the table they form a pattern called an *odum*. The meaning of each odum is based on how many shells fall face-up and how many face-down. Many odums make a word. Each pattern has an exact name and meaning. But these interpretations can't be learned. The word is inspired by the god."

"Do you mean that you were in a trance and that the god was speaking through you?"

"Not exactly. It's a state in which we no longer have real control over what we say, but our consciousness is still clear, which isn't the case in a genuine trance. In a way you hear the design speak. I can intervene, but the message is dictated."

"Can just anyone learn the buzios?"

"It takes a great deal of patience to learn to make the cowries speak, but you learn. You start with four, then eight, then sixteen. Always a multiple of four. You call the gods and they reply. But not just anyone can receive the hand of the oracle. You have to be initiated and have received the imprint of your god."

"Why did you use four shells instead of sixteen some of the time?"

"As I told you, you can never be sure with the cowries. It's good to check some replies. When you use four you get only short, terse answers: four shells face-up mean yes; three mean no; two, the answer is favorable; one, the answer is unfavorable. If you get only face-downs the conclusions are bad."

"Are the cowrie shells used only to identify the master of the head, or do you also use them on other occasions?"

"I consult them every time an important decision has to be made. It may be to establish the most propitious date for a ceremony or for a new initiate's entry into our group, or learn whether this or that magic work will be fruitful. It's forbidden to consult them during Carnival and Lent. And Friday doesn't count as a day for the oracle — except in an emergency of course.

"Once, a long time ago, when the government was persecuting us, the buzios warned me that a police visit was imminent. I immediately hid the forbidden objects of our cult, swept away the drums and ended the ceremony which was in session. At the predicted hour the police knocked at the door. But the buzios had warned me; all I had left were a few crucifixes and sacred images. . . . They found nothing."

"Then there was a time when the government actively opposed Macumba?"

"Yes. It was a stupid decision. I suppose the Catholic Church was behind it all. They must have applied pressure to make our centers illegal. They're always saying that Brazil is the largest Roman Catholic country in the world and that Macumba tarnishes our image. Personally, I don't see how. In any event the persecution didn't last. The gods themselves put an end to it."

"What do you mean?"

"Everyone who raised a hand against us died a violent death. We ourselves are unimportant. But nobody should try to interfere with our religion. Our gods are powerful, and they don't like anybody threatening the source of their strength, their whole purpose in life.

"One day one of our most eminent priests was put in jail. The commissioner who was responsible for arresting him took special pleasure in humiliating him. That very night he was assassinated and our priest was released. It was in all the papers. He shouldn't have made fun of one of our people. It's dangerous to offend our gods. Our gods don't like to kill. But they will if they have to."

"What is your present relationship with the authorities?"

"First we were persecuted, now we're tolerated. Today we exist legally. We're recognized by the government. Terreiros are registered with the police. We even have the right to issue certificates of baptism and marriage which are just as valid as those of the Church. There are still underground terreiros, but they're getting more and more rare.

"In 1941 the First Brazilian Congress of Umbanda met in Rio, and since then there's been a continuing effort to give our cult its proper place in modern Brazilian society."

"Do you use anything else for divination besides cowrie shells?"

"Everything can be used for divination. You just have to pay attention. The universe is full of signs. If you learn to look at things you will understand what I mean. The shapes of clouds, the flight of a bird, the sounds of nature, and unexpected meetings are all messages through which the gods express themselves to us. The universe is a whole which maintains itself, structures itself and evolves in a logical manner. If you penetrate one part of it, no matter how marginal it may be, you can discover all sorts of things by following the chain of cause and effect. You can prophesy and even, if you want, intervene to prevent some things from happening. There are no secrets. Observation is the key to understanding. Each thing leads to the next."

"But if each thing leads to the next, there's no more individual freedom. We're all victims of fate. Isn't that resignation, fatalism?"

"No, my child. Being able to predict gives you a choice.

The situation in which you find yourself is necessarily the result of a previous situation. But the future we move toward is multiple: out of perhaps three or four possibilities it is up to each one of us to choose what's best for us.

"Let me give you an example. Let's say you have a problem. In fact, there are only a few possible solutions to this problem. By using signs you can tell which one will be the best. All you have to do is observe nature's indications — that is divination. There's not one destiny, but many destinies. Which out of all your possible destinies will bring you the most happiness? This doesn't mean that you become what you are not, but that you do not suffer because of what you are, that you *be* it fully. I tell you, you must always respect your deepest nature, you must learn to place yourself in situations which will let you be yourself."

"You told me that I was a son of Oxalá, but then you added 'oldest of the Oxalás.' You also mentioned that each god had several aspects. What exactly did you mean by that?"

"There are three Oxalás, twelve Xangôs, sixteen Oxums, fourteen Omulús, etc. Each god has multiple aspects. Without losing their respective characteristics, they all reveal themselves in slightly different ways. You are the son of the oldest Oxalá, an Oxalá who came long before Christ, who dates from the earliest human times. The older the god the more power he or she has. The gods grow richer with time. That's why the Oxalá aspect is dominant in you.

"Sometimes certain forms of a god disappear in Brazil for lack of a child. It's very sad. But that in no way impoverishes our religion. Let's suppose that one of the aspects of Ogum disappears. It is not all that serious, is it, since Ogum is brought one degree closer to unity and is in fact strengthened.

"A law of equilibrium rules the world; nothing ever really disappears. Someone loses strength, someone else acquires it. Force circulates and changes hands; it centers on one object before penetrating another. But it never runs out. And as long as it lasts, so will our religion. Our cult may undergo certain changes or adaptations, be called by different names or be rejected by a people, but so long as it is accepted somewhere, it will never be extinguished. For it is the very heart of human activity.

"Look at our gods. They've been prayed to under all sorts of names but their essence has never changed. They've had many faces: one day black with frizzy hair, the next day white with blond hair. Look at this statue of Christ — he is Oxalá, your father. Look at this virgin in all her glory — she is Iemanjá, your mother, goddess of the sea. The features can change, but the power never varies."

"I noticed many traces of Christianity in the terreiro — rosaries, figures of saints. . . . And yet you say that the Catholic Church actively persecuted you at one time. How do you reconcile Christianity and Macumba?"

"The Church tried to persecute us, my child . . . *tried*. In the same way long ago white masters punished the slaves who continued to worship the gods of their homeland. They thought they could forbid the entry of our gods into Brazil. They called us instruments of the devil, confiscated our drums and prevented us from holding meetings. The slaves belonged to many African nations, which were consciously dispersed. The Portuguese mixed them all together, hoping to break the ties that held them to their past.[1] In fact, however, this taught us one important thing: that our religions were identical and could be combined into one.

"Then they converted us to Christianity. Christianity is a great and beautiful thing. We learned a lot from it. Most of all it was practical for us: it provided an officially sanctioned form through which we could pray to our own gods. There's nothing wrong with calling Oxalá Christ so long as you recognize his true powers in Christ.

"Brazil is a racial melting pot. We have Portuguese, French, Germans, Japanese, English, blacks from every nation of the western coast of Africa, Brazilian Indians. . . . The true religion of Brazil, Macumba, resembles the people who live it — it has drawn from every source. While it has evolved around a central core which is African, and while its foundation is black, it is always open to outside contributions."

"But how can you maintain that Oxalá and Jesus Christ are one and the same?"

"It's very simple. The Portuguese didn't like to see their slaves praying to black gods. They thought our dances would incite us to rebel. They forced us to adopt Christianity. Our ancestors chose to obey — they had no choice. So they replaced the ancestral figures on their altars with statues of saints. They said, 'Oxalá, give us the strength to stand this life.' And the Portuguese thought, 'What wonderful slaves, all they do is pray to Jesus Christ.' Each god corresponded to a saint, and

[1] In order to prevent the possibility of slave rebellions, the Portuguese never allowed a single ethnic group to dominate in a plantation. This strategy was a success. If, for example, the Bantus decided to revolt, they were invariably denounced by a slave from another "nation."

everyone was happy."

"How were the equivalents between the gods and the saints determined?"

Maria-José smiles. "Oxossi, for example, is the god of the forest and the hunt. His symbol is a bow and arrow. Now Saint Sebastian is shown in Christian imagery with his body pierced by arrows. The relationship was clear: Oxossi and Saint Sebastian became one and the same. The same thing with Omulú. According to our myths Omulú is the god of diseases, particularly of skin diseases. In all the Christian statues of Saint Lazarus he is covered with putrescent sores. So why not associate him with Omulú?"

"I see. But do you believe in the Gospels, in the Bible?"

"I don't know, my son. I've never read them. But I'm a good Christian. I sincerely believe in the strength of the Church, and many of our ceremonies parallel Christian ceremonies."

"Who, according to you, created the world?"

"The gods, of course. But saying it that way is inexact. They didn't create it: they create it every day right before our eyes. They perpetually invent it, every second; they change it, they ceaselessly rework it. You can see yourself that things are constantly evolving. The radio keeps announcing new catastrophes throughout the world, the earth trembles and splits open, mountains collapse, volcanoes erupt, tidal waves drown whole cities. The universe hasn't stopped. It's in continuous transformation. I'm not concerned with the beginning and the end. I'm not even convinced that there was a first day or that there will be a last one. I prefer to consider the motion."

"But don't you believe in a god who is essentially responsible for the creation?"

"I see what you mean. Yes, Olorum is at the origin of things. But he is a very old god. He's so important that he doesn't even bother with us. He's too far away, no one ever calls him. He's like the head of a large factory: the workers address themselves to his assistants or to their foremen; they never have any personal contact with the boss. Olorum is a kind of great boss; the gods we pray to are his children and grandchildren, and we never address ourselves directly to him. He wouldn't even hear us. He's above human affairs."

"With what Christian figure would you associate him?"

"I don't know — with God the Father, or the Holy Ghost."

"How many gods are descended from Olorum? Who are the gods of Macumba?"

"It's hard to answer that question since, as I told you, certain gods returned to Africa. They left Brazil or, in some cases, never came here in the first place. And then it depends on the terreiro. But I can tell you about the gods who come to our center, or at least tell you about their main aspects.

"The essential gods are Iemanjá, Oxalá, Oxum, Ogum, Xangô, Oxossi, Omulú, Iansã. Exú and Ossãe have a special place, as do the Ibejis. The Caboclos and the pretos velhos are spirits, not gods; we don't speak of them in the same terms.

"Each god, who we call an *orixá* in the language, has specific attributes. He or she is linked to a color, an element, a metal, a plant, a human activity, a day of the week, a place. . . . I will tell you about each one of them and indicate these ties."

"Does the word orixá have a meaning?"

"*Ori* means head, summit, skull. *Xa* [pronounced 'sha'] designates a king, a leader. The orixá is therefore the master of the head — dono da cabeça."

Oxalá

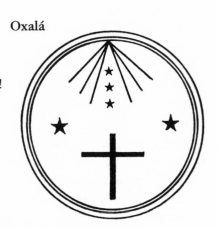

Oh white dove,
little white dove of Oxalá!
Oh white dove,
little dove of Oxalá!
Oh white dove,
little dove of the gods!
Oh white dove,
little dove of the gods!

"I already told you about Oxalá, your father. His color is white, his domain is the sky, his day is Sunday. His activities are mainly intellectual. Aluminum and white gold are his metals. To him we offer a female goat or a white pigeon. He is associated with Jesus Christ."

Iemanjá

I am the daughter of the sea,
daughter of the waves,
daughter of the ocean foam.
Oh my mother Iemanjá,
queen of the salt sea,
oh my mother Iemanjá,
descend and counsel me.

"Iemanjá, whom we identify with the Virgin Mary, is the goddess of salt water. She is very beautiful and lives in a world of luxury and purity among the waves. She wears a great dress of sky-blue satin and a string of pearls; the moon and the stars are her allies. Her own children are not the only ones who pray to her. Iemanjá is one of our essential protectors. She watches over all Brazilians — over everyone who had to cross the sea to come and live here. It's because of her protection that so many Africans were able to survive the crossing in the holds of the slave ships. Still they died by the hundreds before reaching America. All those who escaped death built an altar to the goddess of the sea as soon as they reached land, in thanks for having been spared.

"If you walk along the beaches of Brazil at sundown you'll see hundreds of candles burning in honor of the goddess Iemanjá. They are lit by the faithful seeking her protection.

"December 31st is her feast day. All the terreiros go to the seashore to pay her homage. We gather on the beach and spend the night praising and thanking her. We ask her not to abandon us. We offer her presents and rub ourselves with her water.

"Iemanjá's color is sky-blue. Her children's necklaces are made of clear glass beads. Her metal is silver, her symbol the moon and stars. She likes anything that shines: diamonds, mother-of-pearl, glass. She is, of course, the patron goddess of fishermen.

"When the children want to give her a present, or when they have a special request to make of her, they go to a house of Umbanda where they buy a little silver-painted boat with a metal sail and flag. Inside the boat they carefully arrange white flowers, a tiny flask of perfume, a small cake of soap, a mirror, a comb, and cigarettes of light tobacco . . . everything a woman would like. They tie it all up with blue and white satin ribbons. During the night they go to the beach and launch the boat. If the goddess accepts the gift it is immediately swallowed by a wave and disappears. That's a sign that the wish will be granted. However, if the waves return the boat to shore then the request has been denied; the goddess is annoyed. It is a very bad sign. Sometimes the goddess takes all the gifts but one, sending back the mirror or the soap. In such a case one should not worry. It can simply mean that she feels that particular thing is unnecessary. The wish will still be granted.

"Iemanjá is a strange goddess, at times a disquieting one. She loves her children to the point of forcibly drawing them to her. I remember one of her daughters who was particularly devoted. She was obsessed with the sea. Sometimes she dreamed of it. She would awaken suddenly and tell her husband tearfully, 'My mother is calling me, I must go.' She could not walk along a beach without feeling a desire to enter the water. One day she disappeared. There was a letter on her bed, addressed to her husband. It said, 'The call was too strong. My mother orders me to her side. I can no longer resist. I am going to swim out to find her.'

"The children of Iemanjá should never swim too far from shore. If the sea obsesses them they should immediately see a Mother of the Gods. Iemanjá is also very exclusive in her love, which can sometimes give things a cruel turn."

Xangô

Xangô is quick!
Lightning born.
He lives in a stone
and wakes at dawn.
His little ax is made of gold,
his little ax is made of gold.
With his golden ax
he smashes the evil ones!
Greetings, oh King!

"Xangô is the oldest son of Oxalá and the grandson of Olorum. He is proud, arrogant and short-tempered. He is not a bad god, but he too often acts before he thinks. In his own country he is king. He governs with the help of his twelve ministers, his *obá*, who are also the twelve apostles. There are six ministers to his right — Abiedan, Onikoyi, Aresba, Ohan-Xegum, Tela and Olagbá — and six to his left — Aré, Otum, Nikoni, Eko, Kabá, Ossi-Onikoyi. Today, 'Obá of Xangô' is an honorary title showing great esteem, which is given to distinguished members of certain terreiros.[1]

"Xangô likes warfare and masculine sports. His emblem is an ax or a club. His metal is copper. His color is red. However, the necklace worn by his children is made of red and white beads. Red belongs to him as master of lightning. Xangô is also master of fire.

"Xangô has several wives. When he wanted to marry Oxum, she accepted on the condition that Oxalá be present at

[1]In San Salvador the writer Jorge Amado is an Obá of Xangô from the terreiro of the Gantois.

the ceremony. Now Oxalá was ill at the time; his legs no longer supported him. Xangô carried him to the wedding on his shoulders. Ever since that day white (the color of Oxalá) has been associated with red (the color of Xangô).

"Xangô is synonymous with virility, with masculine strength. He takes care of justice, but that is not his true forte. Oxalá, his father, is often forced to bring him back in line. He can't see a pretty woman without wanting to throw himself at her. It's even said that he raped his own mother, Iemanjá. Xangô is irascible. His anger is terrifying; he spits lightning and burns the land of any person who offends him. Only large offerings can calm his fury. Xangô's stones are meteors, the direct emanation of his power. They are the living stones we nourish in our pejis, the houses of the gods.

"Xangô is associated with Saint Jerome. He is shown as a large, powerful man, and stationed at the entrance to a cave, a club at his knee and a docile lion sleeping at his feet. The lion is a good symbol for Xangô, isn't it? Only Xangô could tame such a fierce animal. . . .

"Xangô is an important ally when it comes to breaking spells. Our terreiro is dedicated to him. He fights off black magic. He punishes evil intentions with his ax. We sacrifice a rooster or a sheep to him. He loves to eat, and particularly appreciates dishes cooked with crab.

"Xangô's day is Wednesday. When the drum beats for him the dances are the lively, syncopated dances of a warrior, a *quebradas*. Sometimes he pretends to take lightning stones from a small bag and throw them on the ground. Sometimes he tries to seduce women in the audience. He is gallant and chivalrous. His feast day is September 30th."

Oxum

My mother Oxum,
Queen of lakes and streams.
My mother Oxum,
hear our prayers!
Near the waterfall
there is a little cave,
near the waterfall
there is a little golden bench;
near the waterfall
my mother Oxum
often comes to rest.

"Oxum is the goddess of fresh waters, of lakes and streams. Just as Xangô symbolizes all masculine forces, she controls all feminine activity. She is physical love, sensuality, femininity, coquetry, jealousy. . . . Her symbol is a fan, a comb or a mirror. If you want success in love you must pray to her. She is given offerings of yellow flowers, a she-goat or a chicken. Her color is yellow, and her metal is gold. She is associated with Saint Catherine.

"Oxum is capricious and fickle, tricky and unscrupulous. She'll use any strategy to keep the love of her husband, Xangô. One day one of his concubines came to her to ask how she managed to maintain such authority over her husband. Oxum replied, 'Oh, Xangô is a greedy man. He likes only the best things. Every evening I cut a little piece off my ear and boil it in water. Xangô adores it.' The concubine went back to her house and confidently cut off her entire ear. When she presented it, cooked and spiced, to Xangô, he gave a jump and furiously chased her off. Then Oxum lifted up her hair to reveal her two ears, both perfectly intact.

"Oxum, who is sometimes confused with Oxumarê the goddess-siren, is the lady of the waterfalls in which we wash our necklaces and celebrate our baptisms. The water of her falls is full of strength which purifies and strengthens the mind. Oxum is greeted with the cry, *Aie, Yeou!*"

Ogum

Ogum is on guard.
He travels down the road
riding his white horse,
a lance in his hand,
a sword in his hand,
riding his white horse.
Ogum is on guard.
Ogum protects me,
he kills my enemies.
Ogum protects me.
He travels the whole world
riding his white horse.

"Ogum is a brave young god, upright and full of fire. A great-hearted warrior, he is associated with Saint George the dragon-killer. It's said that he's a virgin, pure of body and spirit. He is incorruptible, and works only for those causes he deems just. His metal is iron and his color blue. He lives alone, traveling up and down the world to unmask injustice everywhere.

"In my terreiro Ogum is always the first to descend. He's

the first to respond to our call and open the path for the other gods. His symbol is a sword or a sort of wrought iron emblem to which we fasten seven, fourteen or twenty-one small iron points. Sometimes a wreath of palm leaves also indicates Ogum's presence as protector of a place. He's the patron of blacksmiths, workers, farmers and all those who use iron tools in their work — fishermen, hairdressers, and so on. He likes red meat and certain vegetables prepared in oil. He drinks palm wine. His feast day is April 23rd, and his day of the week is Wednesday.

"Ogum reveals himself under a number of different aspects: Ogum Beira-Mar, Ogum Rompe-Mato, Ogum Iara. Under the name Ogum Menino he's a leader of one section of the Indian spirits, the *caboclos*,[1] and fights with Exú to combat evil.

"Ogum is receiving increasing recognition in Brazil. The number of his followers is growing rapidly. He is honored for his courage, his honesty and his efficiency."

Iansã

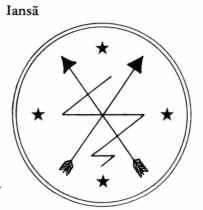

Here comes Iansã
with her luminous crown!
Here comes Iansã
with the wind and rain.
She travels the forest,
flying over hills.
Here comes Iansã,
queen of the wind and rain.

---

[1] The term *caboclo* is usually employed to designate those of mixed black and Indian blood. But in Macumba it is used to refer to all the Indian spirits.

"Iansã, whom we associate with Saint Barbara or Joan of Arc, is a woman warrior, an Amazon. She too was once the wife of Xangô, from whom she stole a talisman that spits fire from its mouth and nose. Like Ogum she lives alone in the sky, armed and helmeted and ready to combat injustice. Her children's necklace is made of red beads. She is storm, tempest and rain. She is the goddess of the River Niger. She likes to dance, her face hidden by the fringes of her crown, holding in her hand a scepter topped with a horsetail.

"Although she's a woman, she often wears men's clothing. She's not afraid to confront the most dangerous powers. She is cold and implacable, and watches over her children like a jealous mother. She destroys everything that gets in her way. She is very beautiful, but she can seem distant to those who do not know her. I'm very fond of Iansã because I know that I can count on her in times of need. She is stubborn, and never gives up once she has undertaken a task.

"Sometimes she is death. She carries off the souls of the dead on her wings. She's the only orixá who dares to confront the spirits of the dead — the *egums*.

"She moves from place to place with the speed of lightning. She is as pure and as luminous as ice. Like Ogum, she is difficult to corrupt. Her feast day is December 4th and is celebrated both inside and outside the terreiro. We sacrifice a chicken to her. We greet her with the cry, *Epazzei!*"

Omulú

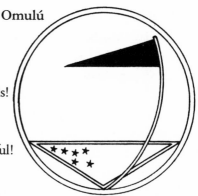

Omulú, hear your child!
You have the strength,
the strength your child needs!
Come to his aid!
You are old
but you are wise and powerful!

"Omulú is the doctor of the poor. All but hidden underneath his straw hood, he can cure all diseases if he wants to. His wisdom and knowledge are infinite. But he is hard to approach. He is suspicious, and guards his secrets jealously.

"Omulú is an old man. As a child he contracted a disease of the skin, and his face is pock-marked. Some people find him frightening, but I think his ugliness is simply his way of keeping nosey people away. He is associated with Saint Lazarus who, like himself, vanquished death. His children's necklace — he has very few — is made of black and white beads. Straw is his attribute. His domain is the earth or the sun. His animals are the billy goat, the rooster, the pig and the dog. He is called upon in times of illness or epidemic, when doctors are powerless to cure.

"Omulú is the leader of the Battalion of the Dead and of the Spirits of the Dead. Cemeteries are his domain. His scepter and hair are adorned with cowrie shells since he, like the shells, holds the secrets of time and knowledge. His powers are infinite but difficult to know. There are secret ceremonies in his honor, closed to non-initiates. Sometimes people make the mistake of describing him as an evil spirit. It's true he sometimes works for black magic when he's associated with Exú, but he usually helps us lift evil spells.

"His day, which is also the day of souls, is Monday. He is sometimes invoked at times of drought or famine. *Atôtô-iê!* is the expression we use to greet him."

Oxossi

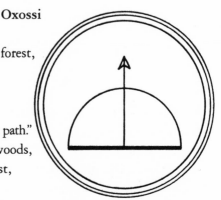

Oxossi is the Indian of the forest,
king of trees and animals,
king of the sky!
King of the Earth!
His arrows show us the "right path."
Oxossi lives in the virgin woods,
he is the Indian of the forest,
king of trees and animals!

"Oxossi or Odé we associate with Saint Sebastian. He is the god of forests, of wild animals and of the hunt. His color is green and his emblem is a bow. He's sometimes called the Captain Hunter, the *Capitão-Caçador*, or the King of the Hunt, *Rei da Caça*.

"Oxossi is the head of almost all the spirits of the Enchanted Forest and of the caboclos or Indian spirits. He always wears green, and always arrives with great feathers on his head, a bow and arrow in his hand and necklaces of teeth around his neck. Are you wondering why Oxossi is the leader of the caboclos?

"When our slave ancestors disembarked in Brazil they were unfamiliar with all the local flora and fauna. And it wasn't the Portuguese who explained it all to them. The Portuguese, my son, had no respect for nature. So our ancestors asked their brother Indians — particularly the Tupinambas. The Indians knew and revered the powers of nature. I think that their religion was not too different from our own. They showed our ancestors the places of power, the virtues of certain plants, the animal species which were useful to human beings. They were their guides in Brazil, this land from which they themselves had been dispossessed.

"Oxossi works with Ossãe, the god of plants. Between them they know all the secrets of healing plant baths, incense and sacred perfumes. Oxossi's day is Thursday. To him we sacrifice a rooster, a pig or a she-goat. He likes corn cooked with coconut. The month of January is dedicated to him. His feast day is January 20th. He is greeted with the expression, *Okê Bambe Ôclim!* Oxossi is the patron god of Rio de Janeiro.

"Blacks and Indians lived side by side for a long time. Their position in relation to the white masters was similar. The Indian sorcerers helped our ancestors overcome the rigors of slavery.

"Brazil is still inhabited by Indian spirits who know the secrets of the forests. We call them the caboclos — enchanted ones. Oxossi, our god of the hunt, is their leader.

"Oxossi descends among us with his bow and arrow to fight against evil. The caboclos also descend into the bodies of our believers. They wear feathers in their hair and paint their faces with bright colors. There are endless numbers of caboclos. The best known are: the Indian woman Jurema, the Caboclo with Seven Arrows, the Rattlesnake Caboclo, the Green Leaf One, the Guarani Caboclo, the Red Stone One, the King of the Forest, the Seven Star One, the Tupinamba Caboclo, and the One of the White Arrow."

The Caboclos

When the forest is on fire
the cabin does not burn.
With his bow and arrow
the caboclo is not afraid of anything!
There where the nightingale sings,
there where the moon shines,
there where my guide stays,
glittering star.
With Oxalá's permission
I saw a caboclo arrive.
He joins in our dance,
the caboclo warrior,
a red cross in his right hand!

The Ibejis

I ask Oxalá
to send us the children,
the sacred twins.
The twins join the dance,
they come to have fun,
they come to take part in our rituals.
I have candy, I have toys,
I have cakes and sodas.
I'm waiting for the twins
to bring me advice . . .

"The Ibejis we associate with Saint Cosmas and Saint Damian. They are twins, sacred children. Their feast day is September 27th but they also appear on a number of other occasions.

"September 27th is the day of all children. On that day they are free to play any game they can invent and no one has the right to scold them. They go from house to house, knocking at each door, and people must always give them a present — candies, cakes, coins or popcorn.

"When the twins descend on a medium, the medium falls back into her childhood. Whatever her age, she acts like a child, crying, laughing, talking in jibberish, grimacing, hopping, sucking her thumb, pinching her friends and whirling angrily around, becoming mischievous and capricious. We give her a lollipop to calm her down. Strangers find the sight of an old woman in an infantile trance grotesque and absurd. But they don't understand us. Some forces of the universe are simply like that: they express themselves in laugh and play. There's no reason to make fun of them. The Ibejis are efficient protectors. Their advice is always very precious. They cure sickness, especially mental disorders. They are the patrons of doctors and pharmacists.

"In our traditional statues you will often see next to Cosmas and Damian a third child, one who does not appear in Christian imagery since he comes from the tradition of our African forebears. His name is Doum. Cosmas, Damian and Doum, the orixá formed by the three of them, is the leader of the battalion of child spirits. The eré, the infantile trance, is their domain.

The Pretos Velhos

Aunt Rosa is an old woman,
a daughter of Bahia.
Aunt Rosa is an old woman.
She knows men's secrets
better than anyone.

"The pretos velhos are the black equivalent of the caboclos. They are the spirits of the old black sages of long ago. They work only for good. Like the caboclos they are typically Brazilian. With their pipes and canes they descend among us to help us. They can descend upon any medium. They are neither gods nor masters of the head; they cannot strengthen us but they can counsel us. They are innumerable; each terreiro has its own. The best known are Father Joaquim, Father José de Aruanda, Aunt Maria de Bahia, Father Joan Batue, Grandma Luisa, the King of the Congo, Father Benedito. . . .

"The pretos velhos are the most authentic expression of Umbanda, for they represent all our powerful ancestors and the history of the black people in Brazil, a history of humiliation, suffering, humility and wisdom. They're the link that ties us to our mother Africa, the link between the first black foot to step off a slave boat and touch Brazilian soil, and the modern Brazilian who prays to the orixás in the center of our great cities. They are all the bound slaves who worked and died on the plantations so that this country could exist. They are our grandmothers and grandfathers who knew how to keep our songs, our beliefs and our knowledge alive under the master's whip, so that our religion could still be alive and still developing today. Where would we be today without the pretos velhos? They are the history and the life of Umbanda. With their hoarse voices and old-fashioned ways, seated on their little wooden benches, Father Antonio and Father Joaquim — and the whole battalion of pretos velhos — will forever be the most vital image of our people's power. May 13th, the anniversary of the freeing of the slaves in Brazil, is the day of the pretos velhos and also the national holiday of Umbanda.

"I haven't mentioned Exú and Ossãe. They are certainly our most important gods. Perhaps the most powerful, and certainly the two without whom our religion could not exist. I'll tell you more about them later. They are the two pillars of our religion."

"Maria-José, what is the history of Macumba?"

"It is long and not very well-known, for our religion often had to go underground. In the beginning our ancestors practiced a religion very similar to the one they had had in Africa. But little by little, due to white pressure but above all because new needs had evolved, it changed. . . . It mixed with Christianity, borrowed certain powers of the Brazilian Indians, came under strong spiritist influences — in short, many of the traits which now characterize Macumba were created here in Brazil."

"How is that?"

"Well, as I told you, Macumba is essentially a recognition of the forces which surround us and the study of the means which allow us to live in harmony with those forces. It's a system which envelops us, structures us, protects us. Anyone can reinvent the system, complete it or detract from it. All you have to do is see, observe and understand. The person who trusts his or her intuitions, who learns to listen only to his or her inner voice, is practicing Macumba without even realizing it. Such a person creates his or her own Macumba. If the system brings results, neighbors will copy it, and a new ritual will rapidly take its place beside the existing ones. Most of our knowledge has come about in this way, empirically."

"Are there any purely African terreiros in Brazil, or have they all undergone a similar evolution?"

"Yes, certain centers have been able to maintain a pure African form. But today they're on their way out. That's normal — they're not adapted to the requirements of modern life. These terreiros are not called Macumba or Umbanda centers, but are known as *candomblés*. They are mainly in the north of the country, especially in Bahia. The most important ones are the terreiro of the Gantois, led by Mother Minininha,[1] and the terreiro of Angenho Velho, both in Salvador.

"The songs of the Gantois — the name comes from the original owner of the house, who was a Belgian — are only in the language. The center is in the Yoruba tradition.[2] It is the oldest and most respected terreiro in Brazil. Many Brazilian celebrities have the honor of belonging to it.

"I know candomblé well, my son, for my mother, whom I succeeded, was a Mother of the Gods who respected the African traditions. But I believe that an overly conservative attitude can only limit the powers of a center. Personally, I accept all influences whatever they may be, so long as they enrich us."

---

[1] Mother Minininha, who in 1972 celebrated her fiftieth anniversary as a Mother of the Gods, is the most famous Mother in Brazil.

[2] Though *candomblés* of every origin (Dahomian, Congolese, Bantu) have existed in Brazil, the Yoruba element has played a leading role. Its theology, religious calendar and rituals influenced all the others.

"You mentioned spiritist influences. How were they able to affect you?"

"A foreigner named Allan Kardec has written on this subject. I haven't read him but I know he's had a lot of influence here in Brazil. In the southern states, mainly in São Paulo, there are even spiritist churches, where they communicate with the dead. The spiritists believe that the dead can help the living. They summon the dead and the dead reply. I've heard that their ceremonies take place in the strictest silence. They don't use drums and they don't dance. I don't understand the source of their powers."

"Aren't the pretos velhos and the caboclos also spirits of the dead?"

"Yes, but not just any dead. No one's going to make me think that all you have to do is die to attain knowledge. . . . I believe that when you die your soul goes back to Africa and nothing is left of you. Still, there are certain people who in their lifetimes attain a certain level of wisdom and accumulate sufficient energy for these qualities to survive them after their death. Their energies comes to rest somewhere and can, in consequence, be invoked."

"What do you mean by 'come to rest somewhere'?"

"I cannot speak to you of that. . . . The mysteries of death must not be discussed. Spirits lodge in nature and, invisible, continue to work by using the bodies of mediums. In the candomblés specialized priests, the priests of the Egums, can also preserve the spirits of certain deceased. The Egums have their own terreiro, on the island of Itaparica, across from Salvador. The spirits are housed in little terra cotta pots. . . . But most spirits find their own resting place. Nature has a kind of memory and is capable of returning them to us.

"You must understand. When a person or a people works in a place they deposit great forces there. The memory of things registers and retains the actions of human beings. Imagine a hill where over a period of years priests invoke the gods and perform magical works. This place will become sacred, a place of powers, which succeeding generations can inherit. I would say that positive energy is rooted there. If a place is a center of black magic for too long it ends up contaminated and becomes cursed and dangerous. Thus, whenever you settle somewhere, always check the identity of your predecessors. And if you have any doubts, be sure always to purify the place before you live there."

"What are the powers of the egums?"

"In the language *egum*, or *egum-gum*, means bone. Because it is inside the bones that the life force is found, and not in the heart or brain as is sometimes claimed."

"Do you mean that bone marrow is life?"

"No, the marrow is its support but it is not the life force. The life force is invisible, locked in the bones, especially in the spine.

"When someone dies, their soul leaves them and goes elsewhere; it becomes hard to control. But it doesn't leave right away. For a while it hovers around the corpse. And it is during that time that it can be rooted. It's difficult to speak about the Egums, because they don't work and don't descend. Their intentions are often obscure. That's why their houses, like those of the Exús, are always placed outside the terreiro."

"Is there an egum house in your terreiro?"

"It's just a little wooden house, my son, no bigger than a

dog house. It is the house of souls. It doesn't contain anything of great interest; just a few small terra cotta pots, a large wooden cross and various offerings which are placed on cracked or chipped plates because they are destined for the dead. At the foot of the cross we light a candle. The little terra cotta pots are like bones."

"What do you mean?"

"They're just little empty pots. They are a substitute for bones. The soul can be contained within them."

"Is there a feast day for the egums?"

"Monday is the day of souls. We light candles for them. But there are also special holidays. Some of them, just after the death of a member of the terreiro, last a whole week. A high mass is said at the end. Others take place every seven years. But all of these celebrations must take place outside the terreiro, for they do not concern life. We always revere the souls of the dead who were members of our center. Their importance varies according to the position they held in our religious hierarchy. The ceremonies are naturally more important for a Mother of the Gods than for a yaõ, an initiate. After all a Mother of the Gods had more powers. And since these powers belonged to the terreiro, it is they that we keep contained in the house of the egums."

"You speak of different positions in the hierarchy of your religion. What are they?"

"I've already spoken of the initiation of a yaõ, of how a medium prepares to receive her god. But there are other degrees of initiation. Over the years the children of the gods may be given increasingly important functions in the terreiro. Their knowledge of our secrets broadens, and they learn to master new powers.

"Some of them become specialists in certain well-defined tasks. They may choose to prepare the offerings, and become cooks of the gods — our gods have very precise culinary tastes. They like this or that cut of meat, prepared exactly this way or that, with a certain vegetable and palm oil or popcorn. Others receive the *mão-de-faca*, the hand-of-the-knife. They become *axogum*, ritual sacrificers of animals; you see, an animal which is incorrectly killed is not accepted by the gods, who become angry and neglect or punish the offending terreiro. Others learn to work with herbs and incense and to prepare the ritual baths and concoctions which give things their strength. Finally, still others may receive the honor of caring for the altar and sanctuaries.

"The level one attains has less to do with age than it does with the knowledge acquired, the powers one has obtained, one's gifts and experience. There is a new initiation for each stage. After seven years of work, for example, the yaõ is confirmed and becomes an *ebane*, receiving new titles and a new name. Later she will learn to organize our dances, lead the chants or direct the ceremonies. Finally, she may become a 'Little Mother,' assisting, or at times even replacing, her Mother of the Gods. Over their lifetimes many initiates who do not necessarily go into trances receive honorary titles which vary according to their power and knowledge.

"These are the godparents, the *padrinhos* of the terreiro. They have a special initiation, but have no 'obligation of the head': that is to say, they do not have to enter a trance or lend their bodies to the gods. They receive the same respect from the faithful and from the mediums as if they were Fathers or Mothers of the Gods. Sometimes they help the terreiro financially."

"Maria-José, how does one become a Mother of the Gods?"

"Generally a Mother of the Gods designates her own successor before she dies. She leaves a kind of will which contains a list of the children in her center in the order of their powers. The first on the list is her successor. If that person dies, the next one takes her place, and so on. Usually it's the name of the Little Mother which is at the top of the list. But the cowrie shells, the oracle, can also speak.

"It often happens that an initiate will leave the terreiro and decide to found her own. Sometimes she's motivated by ambition, and if that is the case the future of her terreiro will never be brilliant. But she may also be obeying the will of her god, who has ordered her, during a trance or in a dream, to found a new center and become a Mother of the Gods. Again, sometimes dissent within a group will lead to a rift and the creation of a new temple. In Brazil thousands of new terreiros are started in this way each year."

"You speak most often of 'daughters' and of 'mothers' of the gods. I noticed that the majority of mediums are female. How would you explain this predominance?"

"It's true there are more women. But this doesn't follow any rule. You must know this, however. On the old farms under slavery, men worked in the fields while women were generally employed in the home. They were maids, nurses, cooks . . . and sometimes even the concubines of the white masters. They were therefore the most influential element of the black community, the least badly treated, and the most capable of preserving their ancestral traditions. In addition, women were always the first to be set free, and so the first to be able to create religious centers.

"Therefore women, perhaps by tradition, play a leading role in our religion. But there is something else. Masculine and feminine power aren't the same. I don't mean that one or the other is superior. No — they are different. Women aren't more intelligent than men, but it's true they understand more. It's not by chance that we are called Mothers of the Gods. Our children know this perfectly well. From the beginning women are more open to trances — they have fewer obstacles in their minds than men. I mean that their minds are always more in harmony with their bodies. You must have noticed that in many people there is almost a break at the neck; the head and the body function independently of one another. This is much less frequent among women; they are of one piece, their bodies are very important to them. When they offer themselves to the gods they give themselves completely, more generously. And so their gift is worth more than that of men.

"Women have a much deeper relationship with themselves than men do. A more direct tie — how should I say — to who they really are. They truly exist on one level, a level of fullness, have less of a tendency to fragment themselves. Look at the way a woman thinks: she doesn't analyze, she emodies. Her vision isn't fragmented. Perhaps that's what's meant by intuition — the capacity to apprehend a person, thing or situation directly, as a whole. Let's say that men, in general, are like surveyors, measuring things exactly, but always on ground level, while women have a bird's-eye view of things.

"It would be too simple to explain it all by the fact that women are the ones who bear children and by the privileged relationship they have with children as a result. The cause lies deeper down than that. I think that women by their very nature, and by that I mean with their bodies, possess the means of penetrating certain realities that men can only guess at. They pass more easily to the other side."

"What do you mean by 'the other side'?"

"There is more than one reality. Humanity knows at least two, but there are certainly others elsewhere in the universe, or maybe even here on earth. For example, a bird doesn't see the world the same way as we do. For us there is the reality of everyday life and that of the gods, spirits and forces that we come to know through, for example, trances. Well, I believe that women are naturally more able to pass easily from one reality to another, to the other side of things. For that is their nature. Men are less malleable, less receptive, less open. They tend to remain only in the reality which has been imposed on them — that of their education, their work, their habits. That's why women make better mediums.

"But there are Fathers of the Gods, although they are often homosexual. There are more and more male mediums and Fathers of the Gods in Brazil. I don't know why — yes, I do have the impression that their number is increasing. But as I was saying, male and female powers are very different, and there can be no terreiro without a certain number of male members since some religious functions can be performed only by men."

"Which functions, for example?"

"Herbs are in men's province — all powerful plants and leaves. Drums are played by men. And in any case, a Mother of the Gods always needs a male assistant, even if only to maintain a certain balance of power. That's why each terreiro has an *ogan* or male assistant."

"Are there relationships between terreiros, or are they all independent of one another?"

"Terreiros are autonomous. The Mothers or Fathers of the Gods who run them are the sole persons responsible for their proper operation: they recognize no superior authority. There are sometimes jealousies or rivalries between terreiros. We all try to gather the greatest number of believers around us . . . but these rivalries never go very far. . . .

"We keep fairly well informed about what's going on in other terreiros. We often invite the faithful of another center to attend our ceremonies. When financial problems become too heavy we help each other out. We all recognize our fundamental identity, our guiding purpose: to help people live better lives."

OPENING THE PATH

Graphic Invocation of Exú:
Exú Curadó

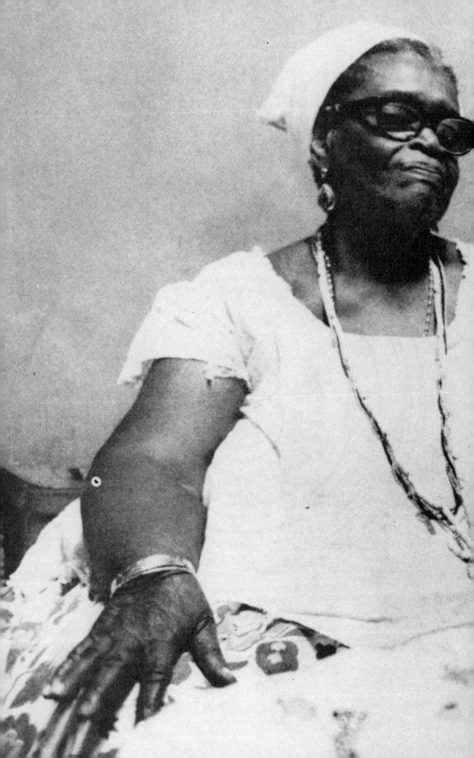

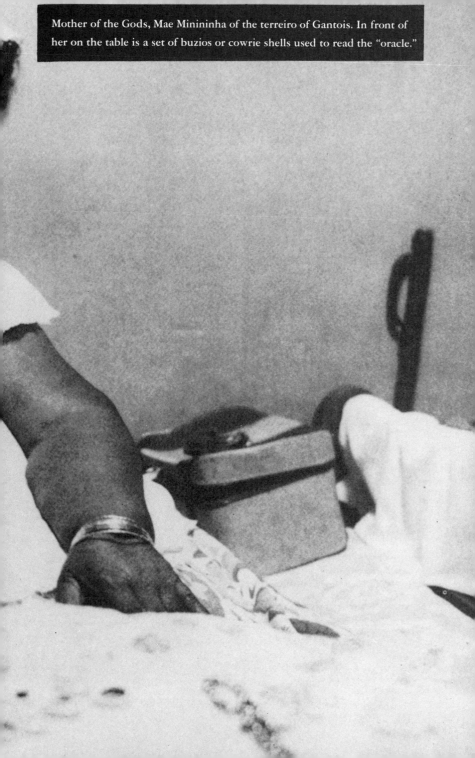

Mother of the Gods, Mae Minininha of the terreiro of Gantois. In front of her on the table is a set of buzios or cowrie shells used to read the "oracle."

The sacred tree of the terreiro of Gantois
in Salvador, Bahia, the oldest and most
respected center of Candomblé in Brazil.

The throne of Mother Minininha in the ceremonial hall of the terreiro of Gantois. On the walls, paintings of the gods, from left to right: Iemanjá, Oxum, Ogum.

Young Father of the Gods in the forest with his two assistants.

A young medium.

A forest offering.

Offering at the edge of a waterfall.

Ringing of the bells during an Umbanda ceremony.

OPENING THE PATH

AT six o'clock in the evening there's a knock at the terreiro door. A man and woman are ushered in. He is white, with greying hair, approximately fifty years old. He wears a well-tailored suit and a tie. The woman is tastefully dressed, her silk dress trimmed with pearls. They advance shyly toward the Mother and kiss her hand. They remain standing. The man seems nervous. He stands with one foot balanced on the other. Maria-José puts him at ease. "I hear you, my son."

He explains that he's the owner of a farm — a *fazenda* — a few miles from the city. He's a cattle rancher, and owns some two hundred acres of land. Until several months ago his business had gone well. He had even been thinking of increasing his livestock and buying up some neighboring land. And then suddenly, from one day to the next, everything reversed itself.

His cows became sterile. The stable roof collapsed, killing ten head of cattle. All his calves died of mysterious causes. The veterinarian could find no explanation, and no trace of any epidemic. All his efforts were in vain. At the moment most of his employees were threatening to quit.

The man seemed disconsolate. Maria-José listened in silence, nodding her head. "How is it, my son, that you have come to see me?"

"A friend told me about you. He told me what you had done for him, how you cured him. He claims my case has something to do with your domain. I've never belonged to a terreiro. But he insisted that I come to see you. Can you do anything for me?"

"I don't know, my son. But I can try. Come back to see me, both of you, tomorrow evening. Bring a black rooster and a box of candles."

Midnight. The candles are burning. The blood of the rooster has been collected in an enameled bowl. The bird is lying on a plate. Its heart, liver, giblets, head and feet have been placed beside the body. We wait outside in the little garden by the kitchen. The Mother approaches, smoking her pipe.

I ask in a low voice to be allowed to witness the procedure she is about to perform. She assents, but warns me that "great forces are about to be unleashed." She explains that a spell has been cast on the man and woman and that she is going to have to summon the gods to get rid of it. "I'm going to extract the evil from their heads and chase it away." And with a smile, "Be careful it doesn't fall back on you!" A little nervous now, I ask whether it might not be dangerous for me to watch the ceremony after all.

She laughs. "I'm a very cautious Mother. Don't worry, my

son; I won't take any risks."

She traces two unequal circles on the ground with a piece of white chalk. She asks the visitors to remove their shoes and to step inside the larger circle. The smaller one, a few yards away, is for me. Across from the man and woman she draws, this time with red chalk, a magic diagram — a ponto riscado.

Her assistant hands her an armful of fresh-cut leaves. She rubs certain parts of our bodies with them — the face, the top of the head, the arms, the legs, the back. Then she swings a small, lighted censor all around us.

The session begins. She places a lighted candle in the center of the magic diagram. Then, arms spread, head thrown back, eyes closed, she begins to pray aloud in a low voice in the silence of the night. Her voice grows stronger and stronger. She calls on Xangô, speaking to him as if he were among us. "Xangô, Xangô, come to the aid of your children. This man and this woman have done no evil, and yet a force pursues them day and night. Look, their animals are dying. Xangô, you don't want their animals to die, do you? Come, they've offered you a rooster and candles . . . you're not going to abandon them. Help me banish from their bodies the evil that has been projected onto them. . . ."

She speaks calmly to the god, with a steady voice and a certain familiarity, as if she were talking to a good friend. She stops occasionally, as if waiting for an answer, then resumes her monologue with a sweet voice.

After a while she opens her eyes, shakes her head to right and left and lights her pipe, which she has stuffed with a special aromatic mixture. She approaches the couple, who have remained immobile and silent all this time, and blows clouds of pipe smoke into their faces, onto their hands, their necks, their shoulders and their wrists. She mumbles prayers. She takes their hands, first his and then hers, and clasps them in her own for a long time.

A bundle of new branches and leaves, different from the others, has been wrapped in newspaper. She shakes them all around the bodies of the man and woman, as if to chase away some invisible presence, to banish it. She motions me to keep still and continues her maneuvers. Suddenly she reaches into a small cloth bag and, taking from it some small brown cylinders, lights a match. She moves so quickly that I don't have time to follow what she's doing. She throws the small cylinders into the air — firecrackers which explode with a deafening sound. She looks at all three of us and smiles. She bows three times toward the ground and thanks Xangô for all the help he's given her. The ceremony is over. Her assistant sweeps away the circles and the magic diagrams. We put on our shoes and the mother offers us some coffee.

As they leave, the man and woman kiss her hand. The man discreetly slips five crisp hundred-*cruzeiro* bills[1] into her hand. Some time later I learned from the Mother that he had come back to thank her; things were back to normal on his farm.

"Men, my child, are too sure of themselves. They neglect to take the most elementary precautions, and if luck smiles on them once, from then on they think they are invulnerable. They plunge ahead without so much as a glance from side to side. They make all sorts of fancy calculations to attain their goals, but they rely only on what they see; they completely ignore the invisible world and their own limitations. They

[1]About $75.

think they're well protected, but in fact they're almost always exposed, highly accessible and vulnerable. . . . They have no defenses, for they place no distance between their image and themselves."

"What do you mean by 'they place no distance between their image and themselves'?"

"Man, my son, is like a beast chained to a post in the middle of a forest. If a wild animal attacks him, he can neither flee nor defend himself, for the chain restricts his movement and holds him prisoner.

"Throughout his life, man attempts to lengthen the chain. He pulls, he pulls hard, he sometimes even adds a link, or two or three. . . . But the chain is still not long enough for him to reach a shelter or resist attack.

"I judge men by the length of their chains. Some of them are so short that the men can barely move. If I wanted to hurt them I would know exactly where to find them: they are there, open, and without defenses. Others manage to move far enough away from their posts to be harder to catch. Finally, some men, and these are unfortunately quite rare, are so skilled at stretching out their chains that they become inaccessible. Seeing them, one no longer sees the chains. Their chains are so long that they are practically nonexistent. These men are the only ones who have no fear: they are out of reach."

"How can one 'lengthen one's chain'?"

"Each link won corresponds to a new step in the knowledge of things. Life is made of 'tricks' or 'recipes' which make it possible to cover yourself a little bit better. Some people work against all odds, others are less effective. But the more winning cards you have in your hand, the more of a chance you'll have in life, right? Except, you see, that there's no book of recipes. . . . Our religion indicates the basic principles and gives the essential rules — but all the rest must be discovered by each individual. You must try, seek, experience failure, find. . . ."

"You told me last night that a kind of spell had been cast on the man and woman who came to consult you. How could you tell?"

"It was so obvious! That man was moving through life without giving the least thought to the waves he was creating in his village. Without realizing it, he was bringing about a whole series of reactions which couldn't fail to bring the roof down on him sooner or later. All the things that happen in this life are related to one another. What you take from one part, you lose somewhere else. This man was piling up successes — he told me so himself — and giving nothing in return. Do you think such a situation could go on forever? The gods were helping him and not receiving their due; they couldn't let that state of things persist. They taught him a lesson."

"But I thought a spell had been cast. . . ."

"Yes. And so?"

"But now you're saying that it was the gods who punished him."

"The gods don't work directly. Their action is revealed only in results. The gods act through human mediation, don't forget that. They themselves do not cast spells. They provoke them. The success of that man must have made people envious. Jealousy piled up upon jealousy until one fine day there was so much of it that it was capable of doing harm. And that's when the problems began for him. The envious ones themselves may not have been aware of the evil they were creating. But a force had been set in motion, and it ended up striking home."

"Then one can cast a spell without meaning to?"

"One almost never consciously desires evil. People aren't bad, my child, it's just that they don't realize what their powers are. I once knew a young woman who wasn't pretentious or arrogant, but who had something about her that bothered people. She was well liked and was generally received with smiles — but envy followed her wherever she went. A vague envy, only vaguely directed at her, but still this young woman had to constantly defend herself against it. No one was consciously attacking her. But she dragged behind her a burden of negative forces which kept growing and growing until it finally weakened her, making her nervous and sick.

"That's the kind of thing that's most difficult to fight. Because it's impossible to locate the evil. This woman was able to survive only by isolating herself."

"Then you believe that mere envy of another person's riches can kill calves, make cows sterile and bring down the roof of a stable?"

"It's not just the envy. It's the whole mechanism that's set in motion. A force is born — which the gods naturally do nothing to hold back — and is unleashed against a person, or against whatever best symbolizes that person, for example, the obvious signs of his success. That man's wealth increased because the gods were with him, but when they withdrew their support his fortune lost its reason to be. And all the negative forces which had been building up against him over the years were able to act upon him without meeting any resistance. If I hadn't intervened, he would have been ruined within a very short time."

"What would have happened if he'd been able to do without the gods' support?"

"Nothing, of course. His business would have continued to prosper. No force in the whole world would have been able to touch him."

"What did you do for him last night?"

"I prayed to the gods, especially to Xangô. I asked them to resume the favorable attitude they had had toward him. I also asked them to accept the presents which were being offered as a token of his contrition. I promised them that from now on he would honor them and that he'd never neglect them again. With their help I was able to extract from him and from his wife the evil that had become lodged in them."

"Why could it have been dangerous for me to attend the ceremony?"

"I freed this man and woman from the evil that was oppressing them and chased the negative forces from their bodies. Once in the air these forces can land on anyone who happens to be nearby and who is undefended. That's why I protected you. I surrounded you with a kind of magic shield. The negative forces could find no easy prey; they were at my mercy, and I dispersed them easily."

"But you yourself had no protection?" She laughs without replying. "What kind of 'magic shield' did you use to protect me?"

"I enveloped you in an impenetrable white circle. I also rubbed you with sacred plants which strengthened you — which, in a way, immunized you from evil. Temporarily, of course. You had nothing to fear."

"At one point you motioned me to remain still."

"You almost moved. If you had, the forces might have noticed you and begun to pursue you. But you were immobile. They didn't even see you."

"At one point you set off firecrackers. Were they special firecrackers?"

"No, not at all. A firecracker is a firecracker. Their only value is that they make a terrifying noise."

"Why is that necessary?"

"They help get rid of the negative forces which are just at the point of leaving the bodies of the people seeking help. When I saw that the forces were ready to give up the fight, to be drawn from the bodies where they were lodged, I terrified them and made them run. I set off my firecrackers, and you saw how they jumped."

"All I saw was the man and woman jumping."

"Yes, but at that moment they were one with the forces that possessed them. That sudden leap of fear corresponds to the precise moment of their deliverance. They too were scared, and their fear brought them back to themselves. You see, I believe very much in the therapeutic uses of fear."

"Do you mean that you can help people by terrifying them?"

"No. Try to understand. . . . Not just any fear. A sudden, brutal, quick, controlled fear. I don't work haphazardly, my child. Man, you see, lives in a prefabricated world. An unreal, deceptive world which has been imposed on him by his culture and his education. He lets himself become imprisoned in the illusory scaffolding which is the world of his ideas. He needs continuously to be brought back to his true nature.

"I always emphasize that we live a false existence: one that we've been forced to live, not that of our deep nature. And that angers the gods, my son, that angers them very much.

"Sweetness, discussion, thoughtful reflection and sermons are no use. They speak to our spirit, they don't affect our whole being. They leave a whole part of us in the dark. Fear, on the other hand, causes instinctive reactions, forcing the inner forces to reveal themselves. It allows you to retrieve yourself, to rediscover your integrity. It rips off masks and transforms a person into a compact block, with no flaws, taut, ready to react — it gives you the vigor of an animal that's been cornered."

"I have to admit it's hard for me to believe in the therapeutic value of fear. It has as good a chance of bringing on total collapse as it does of restoring someone's psychic health."

"You say that because you don't know when or how to provoke fear. The kind of fear I'm talking about never seeks the spirit but only the body. Only intellectual fears are debilitating. Others are restorative. Recently I saw a young man who was severely depressed. He wasn't interested in anything, and life seemed useless to him. He let himself just drift along. The doctors were giving him vitamins, tranquilizers, stimulants. . . . He was holding his own but not improving.

"I talked to him about death. Not of life ending, but of death, of the fact of being dead. I made him so scared that he left here all pale. I also asked him to light a white seven-day candle.[1] A week later he went back to work.

"The candle was for the master of his head. I talked about death in order to demolish the prison of ideas he had locked

---

[1] Candles obtained in a House of Umbanda which burn for seven days and seven nights.

himself into, or, more exactly, that he had been locked into and which had turned him into a passive person. We must destroy the wall of ideas which obstructs our path."

"Am I correct in assuming that you don't believe at all in the value of medicine and doctors?"

"No. That isn't true, my son, that isn't true. I myself sometimes go to a dentist. But what strength can there be in a pill? What energy, what power? A pill has no life. It contains drugs, nothing more. That works upon one part of the organism, but what about the rest? The human being is a whole. If someone has pain in the stomach, it's not enough to bandage the stomach. The sickness may be elsewhere, in the head, for example. You have to extract the illness. Not just calm it and leave it where it is, for it will return sooner or later. It has to be extracted.

"Herbs have strength. Herbs are alive. They are like us. They have their gods and their own existence."

"Last night you rubbed the bodies of the two who came for help with leaves and plants. What kind of plants were they?"

"I don't want to talk to you about them. Plants are our most sacred thing. Without them our religion would be impossible. When I told you the names of our gods I mentioned Ossãe, the god of the vegetable world. Or rather, god of a particular and special vegetable world, the world of powerful herbs."

"Then not all herbs are holy?"

"All herbs *were* holy. Until the day men decided to interfere with their growth. Cultivated plants have no virtue. We never use them in our rituals or treatments."

"Where do your herbs come from?"

"They must be picked far from human habitation, in the

brush or forests — their natural state. Certain species are grown in gardens right around here, but they have no power: human contact has impoverished them. Ossãe is a solitary god. He is the god of virgin land.

"In our terreiro there is a man who is responsible for the cult of Ossãe. He alone knows how to pick the plants, what presents to offer them so that they let themselves be taken, how to keep them fresh and how to remove their roots without destroying their force. He knows which prayers they like, and which holy formulas should be said. He never takes anything without offering Ossãe a present in exchange, some coins or tobacco. . . ."

"How does proximity to humans destroy the power of plants?"

"Man, my child, is a great consumer of energy. When secular life sets itself up anywhere, it feeds on everything it can find — it 'eats' the strength of the earth, uses up the soil, sucks out its strength. Virgin land is like Africa. It's an immense reservoir of energy, and everything born from it is charged with its powers.

"When you walk in a city, no forces enter into you through your feet; the ground is dry and sterile. When you walk in a forest or on a land of power, you feel a great radiance enter into you. It's the force of Ossãe.

"Have you ever noticed that on evenings when we hold ceremonies the mediums dance barefoot on the packed-earth floor covered with fresh leaves? Those leaves come from the forest. They make it easier to enter into a trance. Through them the mediums rediscover the Africa of origins, the pure, living virgin earth of origins."

"Why do you believe that without Ossãe Macumba would not exist?"

"Plants play an essential part in all our activities. Ossãe does not descend — he's omnipresent. Everything we touch, the objects and the holy places of our cult, are washed with special herbs. Initiations begin with the immersion of the god's necklace, and include many washings in soaked plants. Our drums are rubbed with herbs. We ourselves purify ourselves once a week with the leaves of our respective gods. And finally, plants enter into the preparation of our ritual tobacco and almost all the treatments we prescribe to combat spells or illness."

"How, for example, do you prepare plant baths?"

"There are two kinds of bath. The first uses soaked herbs, the second cooked ones. But the ceremony for their preparation is identical. The *cambono colofé* or *peji-gã*, the man in charge of picking them, brings me the plants we need at dawn or dusk. Then a large, clean basin filled with pure water — water from a fountain, a waterfall, sea water, or even rain if it's for Xangô — is brought into the houses of the gods, the sanctuaries. The herbs in the basin are shredded by the hands of initiated women. No stranger is admitted, and the ceremony is conducted in secret. Long ago it was young virgins who carried the bath water, but now it can be any initiated women who do not have their period and who have abstained from sex the night before. Candles are lit, and throughout the ceremony the daughters of the gods sing the canticles of the orixás and clap their hands so that the sound of our songs and the smoke of the candles mingle with the bath water.

"Later, if any water's left over after it's been used, it must be thrown into running water — into a river or into the sea when the tide is falling. If the water weren't disposed of, the work just completed would have no effect."

"You've often mentioned, in relation to the drums, to dancing and now in connection with the baths, that the daughters of the gods could not participate in ceremonies during menstruation, or if they had had sexual relations the night before. Why?"

"My son, the body of a menstruating woman is a closed body. It can receive nothing, for it's already rejecting part of itself. To be a medium is to agree to offer yourself, to open yourself in order to give yourself to the gods. When a woman loses her blood she is ridding herself of a part of her body that is choking her and which must flow out so that she can open herself up anew. But during this period she is in a time of rejection and it is impossible for her to work."

"You can receive nothing from the gods, my child, if you aren't open to them. During a work, for example, you mustn't even cross your legs if you are seated; it would be a negative gesture, an attitude of refusal. The energy can't circulate, and nothing can happen."

"But why the sexual abstinence?"

"For the same reasons. Mediums, whether male or female, must give themselves to the gods, offer their whole being. Before a ceremony no one but a god should have possessed them. But that only applies to holidays."

"Is chastity considered a virtue for the followers of Umbanda?"

"What kind of chastity do you mean, my son? True chastity is a virtue which lies here," she points to her head, "not here," she points to her body. "We want our children to realize their full potential. How could they if they didn't experience sex?"

"Why is there a secret surrounding the cult of Ossãe?"

"Leaves are our power. To unveil their nature would be to weaken them and thus ourselves. It's also dangerous to try to appropriate the secrets of Ossãe without having been prepared to receive them. The man in charge of his cult knows the exact moment and the exact place where his plants should be picked. . . . He knows what he's doing. If you tried to usurp his powers you wouldn't live to be very old, my child. . . .

"You see, everything which has magic powers is like a double-edged sword. Used correctly, the power is beneficient; used without the proper understanding it turns against the careless. . . . The power itself is not well or ill disposed toward human beings: the result depends on how it is manipulated."

"But in all houses of Umbanda you can find a whole variety of prepared herbs, baths and soaps, and no secrets seem to surround their preparation or sale. Don't they have power?"

"Of course they do! But they can't be compared to those which we prepare in the peji of a terreiro, which are penetrated by the force of the gods. I occasionally prescribe them, but their action is limited. They help purify and ward off the evil eye and can make a person feel better. Some of them are applied to the belly, some to the head, some to the whole body. A prayer is said and a candle lit for the god or spirit to which they correspond.

"You can even prepare them yourself. For example, you can pour coarse salt into water and pray to Iemanjá. Then sprinkle your body from head to toe with the water and dry yourself with a new white towel — a towel that's never been used. Then you must put on clean clothes and wrap the towel in white paper — without tying up the package — along with seven white roses. The whole thing should be thrown into the sea. Mondays and Fridays are good days for this. On the beach ask the Mother of the Waters for permission to do this work and throw your offering into her waves as you pronounce your request. Say to her, for example, 'With your permission, Queen of the Sea, I offer you this so that you will grant me peace and prosperity and that I may attain my ideal. Let it be so. *Da licença . . . eu vos ofereço, Rainha do Mar, para que me deiz paz e prosperidade e realize o meu ideal . . . Assim seja.*'"

"I've often heard it said that you use hallucinogenic plants and *maconha* [*cannabis indica*, a form of marijuana] in your preparations."

"My son, each god has his or her own plants. Ossãe is the master of them all, but each plant is consecrated to a particular god. Those which are used to wash your necklace are different from those I'd use for a son of Ogum or of Iemanjá. So even if I used maconha, it wouldn't be systematically incorporated in our cult; as for the idea that our trances are induced by drugs, it's obviously absurd. Our gods have no need of drugs. They're powerful enough to descend all by themselves, without resorting to such a gross artifice. . . ."

"In general your plants are reserved for external usage; you rub the body with them. You wash yourselves with the water in which plants and herbs have been soaked. How does the power of the plants actually work?"

"I told you that our plants are alive. The contact of life never fails to produce an effect. . . . Let me explain it to you. I knew a man — he died a long time ago, may he rest in peace — and people came from all over to consult him, since contact with him was enriching. They sat down next to him, asked him a question, and he'd take hours to answer. And then they left, feeling restored. This man was convinced that his intelligence — the accuracy of his observations and the common sense of his advice — were the reason for his popularity. He spoke like this from morning to night with a steady stream of visitors entering his tiny room. One day when he was already old he fell sick. His throat began to hurt and he lost his voice. Yet his room did not grow empty. The visitors were just as numerous as before. At first he thought they were coming only out of sympathy for him. But then he realized that the people were leaving his room with the same smile of pleasure as before. And he understood that words had no importance, that mere contact with him was enough to create a sense of well-being in those who came to see him. From that day on until his death he preached no more. He gave no speeches, but simply stayed in his corner, receiving his visitors with his usual good humor. And his popularity continued to grow.

"The same thing is true of our plants. The essential thing is the contact, the presence. There are mediums who heal people simply by laying on hands. They touch a wound with one finger and it immediately closes up and forms a scar. They know nothing of medicine, and do not even think about what they are doing: they let their powers take over.

"I can't explain to you why or how our plants work. I can only tell you that our priests, over the centuries, noticed which plants produced positive results when brought into contact with which sorts of people. Our religious practice developed on the basis of that kind of positive evidence.

"There are powerful people, just as there are powerful plants and powerful places. . . . We're committed to finding out who they are and using them for the greater good of everyone. . . ."

"You already mentioned powerful places. How can they be recognized?"

"The power of things comes from the gods, and thus from the powers of nature. When you see nature expressed with unaccustomed violence in some place, you can be sure that there is power there. Waterfalls, for example, are the domain of Oxum; the higher and bigger the waterfall, the greater the presence of her powers.

"For us the shapes of mountains and stones, the markings on a tree, the size of the waves in the ocean, the speed of wind or the trajectory of a cloud are not without significance. Perhaps you've noticed that several miles from here there is a giant rock which bears some resemblance to a man. The site itself is extraordinary. People say, 'What a gorgeous landscape!' They speak of its beauty, thinking only of the pleasure to their eyes and spirits. But it has nothing to do with beauty; the feeling of pleasure that arises in people who go there has nothing to do with the esthetic qualities of the place but rather with the powers and the strength that are released *by* it.

"I understand that the idea of power and strength is confusing. But just because a thing is difficult to understand is no reason to deny its existence or to be content with a poor explanation. To speak of beauty in describing certain landscapes is deceptive. It's a kind of sorcery of the spirit which attempts to account for something beyond its comprehension. But nature isn't 'beautiful' or 'ugly'; it is charged with forces or insipid. And the gods aren't artists. They generate energy in its raw state!"

"But what about residential places — houses?"

"A house is something else. It is not there to nourish but to protect. And we have to guarantee that protection. The embellishments have been placed here by human hands, so their value is only decorative. A house has to have openings. These are its weak points. They are so many passages through which negative forces may enter. Our religion teaches us to defend them."

"What do you mean?"

"Our followers often call us to their homes to bless them. But they themselves usually know how to keep bad influences at bay. These things are part of our tradition. I don't understand how you can be unaware of them."

"In my country people are content to lock their houses with a key."

"Thieves are one thing, my son, but forces are another. Forces can pass through a locked door with no trouble at all. 'Door' to them does not signify a solid piece of wood, but an area of passage, a will of opening, a possibility of circulation, entry.

"Our faithful know that a house, the place where one lives, must be regularly purified. They buy the special incense or *defumador* of their god and spread its smoke in all the corners where evil spirits might be hiding. Windows, entrances, corridors, nooks and crannies and rooms which are rarely used all deserve special attention. The person holding the censer must maintain absolute silence throughout the procedure. The least word would annul the effect of the work. The person must concentrate on what he or she is doing, not think of anything else.

"There are as many defumadores as herbal baths, and each

of them must be used its own special way. Generally speaking, people begin in the farthest room of the house, apartment or store and proceed toward the entryway or street. This gets rid of the evil influences. Before anything else is done it is best to light three candles and to ask the god's permission to perform this work. Then several prayers should be said. You might say, for example:

> Who comes, who comes,
> who comes from so far?
> It is the tiny angels
> on their way to work.
>
> Oh give me the strength,
> for the love of god my father!
> Oh give me the strength
> to be able to work!

"Then you fill your censer with the proper defumador, which can be bought in a house of Umbanda, and cover it with burning embers. You balance it gently in your right hand, while in your left you hold a glass of clear water. When the work is finished you throw the glassful of water out the front door, as far as possible from the threshold; all the evil influences that may have been in your house will disappear with the water. Sometimes the ashes that are left in the censer should be placed at night at the intersection of two streets, wrapped in white paper and accompanied by various offerings — candles, cigars, liquor, matches and yellow manioc flour — *kfarofa amarela* — which has been cooked in palm oil.

"Defumadores play a very important role in our religion. Before each dance session the terreiro and all participants in the ceremony are covered with incense by the *cambone*, an assistant to the Mother who has been assigned this task. The purifying power of the smoke is great.

"But that is not enough. Once purified, the house or apartment must also be protected from the evil eye. Somewhere near the door of each Brazilian home there is a *figa*, you know, one of those fists of wood, stone or metal — it doesn't matter which — with the thumb between the index and middle fingers."

"Figas are also sometimes worn around the neck, as jewelry. What is their origin?"

"The figa is an old African protection derived from a gesture that was used to chase off the evil eye. Whenever our ancestors felt that a spell was going to be cast against them, they clenched their fist, allowing only the thumb to be seen between the index and middle fingers. When they disembarked in Brazil for the first time, they had no idea where they were: they walked off the slave boats, their bodies weighted down with chains, making the sign of the figa to protect them from this land of exile. Ever since then the figa has been universal in Brazil. Some are made of gold, others of precious stones. They are sold in jewelry stores and as souvenirs for tourists. But the price you pay for a figa has nothing to do with its real worth. No matter how luxurious your figa may be it's worthless unless it has been blessed — washed — in a terreiro."

"What other means of protection do you have?"

"The figa is a concrete object which anyone can hang on a wall. But if you feel very threatened it isn't enough. Sometimes I have to advise certain of my followers to stick a sharp knife or a pair of scissors in their door. This breaks the spells or evil forces that might try to cross the threshold of their houses.

"Exú is a faithful guardian, but I'll speak of him later. There are two ways to get rid of a spell. You can combat it with a superior weapon that will break or annihilate it, 'cutting' its power. Or you can force it to make a detour onto something else, a kind of scapegoat — either a sacrificial animal, a fruit, an object, or the head of the person who originally cast the spell.

"The figa, scissors and incense belong to the first category. For more serious threats — illness, bad luck, death . . . when the path is truly closed — you have to use the detour method."

"What are the powers of scissors and knives?"

"No, you don't understand. These objects have no power. They represent something; they are weapons. When evil influences or bad spirits see them, they are frightened, since they know they are in the presence of a protected place. They dare not enter.

"To sink a sharp knife with a good cutting edge into a front door is a gesture of defiance, symbolic perhaps but still a message of aggression, and the spirits are sensitive to it, it discourages them. They understand that the owner of the place is not about to let it be invaded. They are afraid, and they run off. It is a way of intimidating them."

"Maria-José, how do I know if I'm the victim of an evil influence?"

"But, my child, everytime things go wrong! I'm going to tell you something." She moves closer to me. "Influences, evil forces, enter us through the head and the stomach."

"What do you mean?"

"I already told you that doors, windows and all the openings of a house are its weak points. Well, people's heads and stomachs are *their* weak points. That's where we're most vulnerable. In a way, human beings are double: the head may govern us, but it takes its cues from the stomach. The former is the organizer — the past, origins, friendship, knowledge. It is sensitive and fragile, as you can notice. If you touch the head of a medium in a trance, either with your hands or with some impure thought, you can practically drive her crazy or even kill her. The stomach, on the other hand, is the seat of all the forces that permit you to advance. That's where we find the forces that are rooted in nature. That's where they are stored. The will begins in the stomach." She points to her solar plexus. "Here!

"Negative forces make the mind become disorganized and vague, depriving their victims of their sense of unity. Or they can tie their victims' stomachs up in knots, pressing in on them so that they feel blocked. If you ever feel threatened by such forces, breathe deeply through your stomach with your eyes closed, and tighten your abdominal muscles as hard as you can on every inhalation. This will create a barrier through which the evil forces cannot pass. Or, if you wish, still with your eyes shut, hold your breath and rest your tongue on the upper surface of your palate until your brain feels like a large, compact ball, a solid stone resting in your skull.

"This is how a person at the height of her powers and possibilities should feel: like a living rock, a single mass which nothing can crack."

"Maria-José, you've given me a number of recipes for self-purification, self-fortification, and for freeing myself from evil influences. Many of them are very complex and call for specific offerings. For example, you said that there are hundreds of different baths, hundreds of kinds of incense and hundreds of sacrifices, and that they also vary depending on the god they are intended for. How do your followers know which ones to use?"

"My child, in any drugstore you will also find hundreds of medicines, each with instructions for its proper usage, dosage and with a word of caution. Some of them are familiar to you and you don't need a doctor to obtain them for you or administer them. The same thing holds true in our religion. You are a foreigner, but our followers know many of our methods simply through habit or tradition. Sometimes, however, they need the opinion or advice of a medium or of a Mother of the Gods. I tell them the correct way to proceed, where to place their sacrifice, how many candles to light, which prayers to say, and so on. There's nothing mysterious about it. All they have to do to open a path or keep it from closing is obey us to the letter and follow our instructions."

"You often use that expression. What do you mean by a 'closed' or 'open' path?"

"Life, my son, is like a path that winds around a hill. When everything is going well you can proceed uninterrupted toward the top. Your path is open. But when too many negative forces pile up against you they obstruct your path. Your possibilities in life are reduced to zero. There is no future for you. You are blocked. And if no one agrees to open your path you will simply disappear, I mean you will die.

"Fortunately things sometimes resolve themselves by themselves. You have a spell of bad luck and then, little by little, things return to normal. Usually you don't even pay attention to these things; you simply say, 'I just don't know what's wrong. Everything's going from bad to worse.' You don't really worry until this sort of situation appears permanent.

"If things do resolve themselves sometimes, it's because our positive forces have won out over the negative. Unconsciously we set in motion a whole system of defense; in addition, there may be enough people around us wishing us well. In the balance of things, this weighs in our favor.

"Sometimes, however, our luck doesn't change. Then we have to consult a person capable of opening our path. It's important not to delay. Inaction and passivity work against us. Bad gets worse and becomes more deeply rooted in our heads."

"What do you do to open a path?"

"Last night you saw the gods break a spell. Xangô fought the evil with his golden ax. He opened the path. The treatment varies depending on the form the evil takes. But, as I said, most of our followers already know how to solve their problems.

"One of the more radical solutions is to transfer the evil somewhere outside you. There are statues that can be decapitated, fruits that we let rot, animals that are allowed to die. For example you might buy a small animal, let's say a turtle, and have it blessed. You rub it against you and then stop feeding it. When the turtle dies the evil disappears with it."

"And if it continues?"

"Then you should consult me. [A silence] You think all this is nothing but superstition, don't you? That we're just a bunch of poor, ignorant Brazilians, terrified of everything, who let innocent animals starve to death out of sheer stupidity, right?

I can tell exactly what you're thinking. Then listen to this.

"Life isn't what you think. And 'reasonable' intelligence doesn't necessarily bring happiness. Life is a dangerous game, and the rules weren't established by human beings. You want to join us — fine! Then take off your blinders! Stop looking only at those aspects of the world that are convenient to you, and look at the totality! When you present the facts don't interpret them, because all you do is distort them. Your culture and your education are ruining you, my child. I don't know the country you come from, but I have the impression that the people there are very alienated from their roots. . . .

"Animals know better than you do what I'm talking about. I'll give you an example. When one of our followers wants a favor from her god, an offering, a despacho is made, accompanied by candles and prayers. There's a waterfall several miles from the city. Go there, and you'll see how many despachos there are. Among the cigars and candles there are many large ceramic plates piled high with food — popcorn, chicken, rice, all sorts of good things. This food is reserved for the gods. People wouldn't touch it for anything in the world. That's natural, you'll say; they are afraid. But there is something else. Lost dogs, starving and bony, wandering at night along the edge of the cascade, come up to these heaped platters, sniff the food and walk away. [I verified this myself following our conversation.]

"How can you explain this? Why do the dogs prefer to go hungry rather than touch what has been offered to the gods? You can't think of an explanation? Because they know that hunger is preferable to death. That the gods would quickly punish anyone who touched their food. The dogs sense this, and that's why they run away. But go ahead and say that Brazilian dogs are superstitious, if you prefer that explanation."

"Maria-José, how can such simple, inoffensive objects as cigars and candles change the course of our life? There's such a gap between the problems and the solutions you suggest, between the end and the means."

"Once again you think that way because you're mistaken about the true nature of things. To you a candle is only a piece of wax with a wick down the middle. But tell me, my son, is a candle lit during a blackout and a candle offered to a god exactly alike?"

"Of course I think differently about them, but in fact they are identical."

"That's where you're wrong, my son. One is filled with your hopes, the other with your anger at being left in the dark. What really counts is what you put into things. Human beings are not aware of all their powers. Not a single gesture you make is without consequence, without effect. Every motion, every action, has invisible repercussions which create a presence that surrounds you. One day this presence which you create by yourself will reveal itself to you in broad daylight.

"It's odd, you have no problem in accepting the existence of ideas such as liberty, will, and so on. But you can't understand the idea of power. Yet right under your nose every single day are examples of relationships between forces and their results. I suppose it's primarily a question of vocabulary. You were taught to classify things under a certain label, and now you no longer see the things themselves."

"But Maria-José, when you describe these mysterious, supernatural forces, you. . . ."

"You see, my child, you see? You say 'mysterious, super-natural forces,' but our forces aren't the least bit mysterious — they are the most natural thing on earth! Your vocabulary is hurting you. And then you over-complicate everything. Have you noticed that contact with certain objects has the power to depress you? Have you ever felt ill at ease in certain places? Have certain friendships diminished you? And how did you explain the uncomfortable feelings you had on such occasions?"

"I don't know . . . things just depressed me. . . ."

"A place is depressing because it depresses you. That's not too impressive, my son. . . . When you find yourself in the presence of negative forces, your own forces — everything that is most positive in you — join together to fight for equilibrium. You necessarily lose something in this fight. You always end up weakened. You strive to maintain your identity in the face of what's conspiring against it, and this effort is the source of your anxiety.

"The world is active, my child, it's never neutral. It's always for you or against you. You must learn not to spend your energies in vain. Always be in a position of strength. Learn to recognize yourself in all things.

"Human beings are above all great consumers of energy. Do you believe in vampires? I saw a movie on television in which one man sucked the blood of another. If you think of blood as the essential source of energy, the image makes sense. People spend their time sucking up each other's energy.

"There was a good medium in my terreiro, a young woman who possessed great powers. One day she got married. And little by little her gifts began to diminish. Finally she had to stop participating in our ceremonies. She came to see me about a year ago, a real living corpse. I thought again of that movie. The woman seemed to have been emptied of her blood. She wanted my advice. Her husband was cheating on her and threatening to leave her. She was ageless; she had been stopped in time. Her eyes were haggard and expressionless. She could no longer sleep at night. She stuffed herself with sleeping pills."

"What did you do for her?"

"Some people, both men and women, belong to the race of vampires. In other words in order to survive they're forced to feed on the energy of others. Not out of bad intentions, and not in order to do evil. Much worse: out of necessity. The husband of this woman had in fact 'lived off her.' He had sucked her dry of all her forces. Now that she was empty he had turned to another victim.

"I washed the woman. I purified and strengthened her. Two of our initiates took her to a spring near our terreiro, up on the hill, where they soaked her head in running water. We sacrificed a she-goat on her body, rubbed her with the herbs of her god, and brought her back to herself. We brought her back to life.

"We had to treat her like a child. She was dead and had just been reborn. We re-taught her the simple motions of life — eating, drinking, sleeping. Today she is once again a happy woman."

"And her husband?"

"Oh, for him it was different. I asked him to come see us. At first he was terrified, but he was afraid to disobey a Mother of the Gods." She smiles. "He could see the changes his wife was undergoing, and he thought I must have something to do with it.

"One afternoon he finally showed up. I explained the situation to him. His wife was a daughter of my terreiro, and I had had to intervene in order to protect her. I told him that I could either cast a spell on him and block his path so that he'd be incapable of doing further harm — in which case he wouldn't be long for this life — or I could treat him in my terreiro and teach him how to use the vital energy he had within him. Naturally he chose the second possibility.

"He came once a week. Eventually he was initiated and everything went back to normal."

"What happened to his mistress?"

"His wife knew exactly what to do to get rid of her. She placed a drop of menstrual blood in a strong cup of coffee and offered it to her husband. He drank it, and from that moment on he never looked at another woman again."

"Before I came to see you, I had the impression that your role was limited to large public ceremonies. I didn't realize that you also entered into the private life of your followers."

"My child, belonging to Macumba doesn't mean you simply come to see our dances and hear our chants. Macumba is a complete religion; I mean, a system of ideas and practices capable of intervening and helping us at every moment of our lives. Otherwise what would be its value?"

"At about what age does your religion begin to play a part in a person's life?"

"But . . . from birth, of course. Before being blessed at the church in the presence of their godparents, the children of our followers are always brought to us. We have special leaf baths for the newborn, just as we do for all the different stages of life

— puberty, marriage, death. . . .

"We do more than just bless the baby. The buzios, the oracle, have their own opinion to offer. They announce the precautions to be taken, and foresee the treatments that should be applied. They occasionally oppose a marriage and denounce those they consider incompatible. Some of our gods don't get along well with each other. If their respective children were to marry the results would be catastrophic. Unless, of course, the proper sacrifices were performed. . . .

"Macumba takes care of its followers from birth to death. It prevents the faithful from ever being alone, and it supports them at all times, against all adversaries. It can operate anywhere, under any circumstances. It excludes no one. All of us can be its children."

EXÚ

Graphic Invocation of Exú:
Exú do Cheiro

Greetings of the drums.

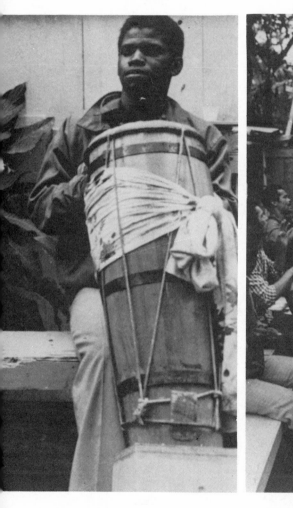

The Mother of the Gods greets the ogans, the male members of the terreiro.

Dancer.

Greetings to the Mother.

Offerings to the caboclos, the Indian spirits.

The caboclos, the Indian spirits, come out of the inner sanctuary.

The Mother of the Gods calms a turbulent god.

A medium is brutally possessed by a god.

Session aimed at countering a "work" of Quimbanda, of black magic: around the "victim," the mediums enter into trances and a circle of fire is drawn.

Healing ceremony in the woods.

Full-size statues of Exú and Pombagira.

Pombagira.

EXÚ

IT is late at night. I'm driving through the suburbs of the city. Houses and empty lots give way to one another endlessly; the mountains and the forest are nearby. I've left the friends with whom I spent the evening. The way home had seemed simple enough when they explained it to me, but now I have the distinct impression I'm lost. I've been going around in circles for fifteen minutes without being able to get back on the main road. I'm in a brand-new, deserted neighborhood without street lamps or street signs. There's no one around to help me. I accidentally enter a dead end street. I start to make a U-turn when I notice some lights off to my right, at the end of a wooded piece of land about a hundred yards away. I stop the car and get out to ask directions.

The scene that awaits me is not at all what I expect. Within an enclosed rectangular space marked off by several wooden posts — the posts are trimmed with red and black ribbons and their tops are joined to one another by lengths of cord — three people are 'working' silently by candlelight. There is a fairly pretty woman about thirty years old wearing a long skirt, a puff-sleeved blouse and a red turban; a graying man, clearly her assistant, who obeys her by bringing in various ceremonial objects at the appropriate time; and a man in dark clothes with his hands crossed behind his back. Only he seems bothered by my sudden appearance. Before I can even say a word, the woman imperiously motions me to be silent. She directs me with her gestures to the entrance of the enclosure, asks me to take off my shoes — she is also barefoot — and bids me join them in the center of the small terreiro. She rubs me with herbs, pushes me into a corner, and again motions me to be quiet. I decide I had better be obedient and wait.

The woman draws a circle in the ground with a wooden stick. Then she presses some small pieces of metal into the earth and places a large bowl of blood in the center. I notice a dead animal, a black rooster, in a corner of the terreiro. The woman is smoking a cigar. Her assistant offers her a bottle of cachaça, which she empties on the ground all around the bowl of blood. Next to the bowl she also places two cigars, one on top of the other in the form of a cross. She unseals a new box of matches, opens it, and slides seven matches out just far enough so that the match tips are protruding from the lid. She closes the box, leaving the match tips visible, and places it on the ground beside the cigar-cross.

The assistant takes a small drum from a gray cloth bag and begins to beat it rapidly. He chants:

I call you at midnight,
I call you at dawn.
Come to the people of Quimbanda!
Exú eh, eh, eh
Exú ah, ah, ah.

The woman lights seven new candles, each with a different match taken from a different brand new box. She places them around the bowl of blood. She asks the well-dressed man to give her back "you know what"; he takes from his pocket a small package, which she takes and buries in the ground in front of one of the candles. She marks the place with a cross and blows on it with her cigar smoke.

She begins to drink. She gulps down alcohol as if it were milk. In three mouthfuls she has emptied the bottle. The drum continues pounding. She dances, making sweeping gestures. The well-dressed man does not move, but looks downward, his eyes fixed on the ground.

She stumbles — her legs seem barely able to support her. She bursts out laughing and in obscene language tells her assistant to be quiet. Large drops of sweat roll down her forehead. Her features are distorted by a nervous tic which causes part of her face to quiver. She spits on the ground, and, grimacing, launches a prayer. She asks "the god of hell" to grant her desire. She says, "Look at the beautiful presents that await you, Exú — blood, alcohol and black cigars! If you take them, it's a sign that you agree to help me. Well then, Exú? The cigars are good. The alcohol is strong. Are you hesitating? No, of course not!" She bursts out laughing again. "He has accepted," she murmurs. And she asks her assistant to resume his playing.

She turns toward me. "You, now you may leave. Not like

that, imbecile! Backwards! Leave here backwards. Put on your shoes and turn around, and leave without once looking back at us. Do you understand? Don't look back until you've gone at least half a mile from here!"

I leave just as she tells me to. I get back in my car and take off as fast as I can. This time I find my way without too much trouble. I don't let up until I'm safe inside my house; then I breathe a sigh of relief.

> Here is Exú,
> midnight Exú
> Exú of intersections!
> Here are Exú and his wife,
> the lovely Pomba-Gira!
> He's wearing his black cape
> he's wearing his black hat
> he's wearing his polished shoes.
> With his iron trident in his hand,
> Here is Exú
> midnight Exú,
> Exú of intersections!

Maria-José laughs at my adventure. "You saw the devil! The devil at work! Exú, king of black magic and Quimbanda!"

"What's the difference between Umbanda and Quimbanda?"

"The followers of Quimbanda use the same principles as we do, but they seek only to do evil. They pray to the Devil to assist them in their evil projects; they cast spells, send illness over great distances, even cause death. . . . The priests of Quimbanda work with the left hand: they will cause the most horrendous things to happen, all for money. Our job is to combat them. The police are powerless against them. They have no way to fight them. But we, the Fathers and Mothers of the Gods, use all our knowledge to chase away evil."

"Why did that woman allow me to observe her ceremony?"

"She had no choice. You arrived at the beginning of her invocation. You had to follow it until the end. Otherwise she would have lost a part of her power. She protected you with herbs; she wished you no harm."

"Why did she force me to be silent?"

"Because Exú was about to appear. You could have said something in and of itself quite harmless, but which the god might have interpreted differently. And most of all you would have broken the 'charm.'

"Exú isn't easy to summon. I don't mean that he's reluctant to descend, but we're never sure what's going to happen with him. He's capricious and rebellious. When summoning him one has to proceed with caution. Silence is the best precaution."

"What did the man in dark clothes want?"

"I don't know . . . but it couldn't have been anything too good. You said the woman buried a small package that he gave her. That's your answer. It could have been almost anything — hair, a shoe, a personal object, papers, photographs — anything. But what is certain is that the victim will be the actual owner of the contents of the package.

"The well-dressed man is the one responsible. He approached a Quimbanda priestess and asked her with total impunity to help him commit his crime. Perhaps he closed off someone's path; maybe he sought someone's death or ruin. It's impossible to say.

"In any case he must have robbed some personal object from

the man or woman he was trying to harm. Then he gave it to the woman in red who agreed to work for him, in return for cash.

"People are often killed like that in Brazil; without a knife or gun, by the simple power of these forces. Our slave ancestors got rid of many a white master in that way. They would say, 'Let's work with Exú to sweeten the master.'

"Black magic is just as valid as white. From the moment when people learned to control the forces of nature, they used them in both directions. People aren't evil; they simply seek to improve the conditions of their lives. This becomes serious only when their personal advances are at the expense of someone else. That's all."

"What will happen to the victim of the spell that was cast last night?"

"How could I know, my son? I told you — maybe death, maybe sickness, perhaps a gradual decline. . . . It's sometimes possible for the victim to notice in time to save herself. I hope that's what happens in this case."

"What could the victim do?"

"Either consult a Mother of the Gods, or else go see a Quimbanda priest who will not only lift the spell but make it descend on the person who originally cast it — punishing evil with evil. Why worry about it? It's useless. And then of course it's always possible the spell won't even affect the person. . . ."

"What do you mean?"

"Well, if the victim's sufficiently well protected, positive forces will arrive to defend her, on the heels of the negative ones sent. Everything depends on the person's degree of permeability and accessibility. Life is a battle of forces.

"Followers of our religion have at their disposal a whole system of defenses. This set of protections works like lightning rods. The lightning still strikes, but instead of killing someone it's captured by the rods, which divert it into neutral ground."

"How can you tell whether you're at the center of a battle of forces?"

"But we are always at the center of a battle of forces! There's no peace, no respite. The struggle (or call it a game) doesn't stop until you die. So long as you're living, nothing's definitive. You never eat once and for all — you have to eat every day, right? You exhaust the value of what you consume very quickly. The same thing's true with forces, all kinds of things weave their way around you. What you're seeking is energy, which you accumulate and then expend. You use up your reserves so you can advance and defend yourself, then the cycle starts all over again."

"Could I have intervened last night? Could I have done something to prevent the spell from being cast?"

She laughs heartily, "Of course, of course. You could have offered to take the place of the designated victim . . . and played the part of a lightning rod. But that wouldn't have kept the well-dressed man from starting all over again as soon as you'd left. If you're not very, very powerful my son, don't get involved with magic. Especially not the magic of others. From now on if you ever hear Exú being invoked, do exactly what the woman told you to do yesterday: go your way and don't look back. A single glance behind you will put you in a position of weakness and vulnerability."

"Why did the woman ask me to leave the circle backwards?"

"When Exú becomes the Devil, he does everything in reverse. His gestures are the opposite of what they would normally be. Sometimes he makes fun of the Catholic mass; he parodies the priests, transforms the words of the prayers into nonsense, and takes communion with the blood of a rooster.

"But you were asked to leave backwards for another reason too: to make it seem as if you'd never been there in the first place. I already told you that things and places have a kind of memory. When you enter a closed place, part of you becomes attached to it: you lose something of yourself there. You have to learn how to leave in such a way that you don't lose a single fragment of your being. Yesterday was an especially serious occasion. You had to erase the whole lapse of time from the moment you arrived in that terreiro. By following your own footsteps in reverse you in effect annulled the fact of having come there. Even when you go to a friend's apartment, you should always leave through the same door you enter. Never through another. You would be diminished. Learn to move without leaving a trace.

"Those who don't follow these rules spend their time undoing themselves, dislocating themselves. Little by little they gradually lose themselves. It's very hard for them to maintain their wholeness, they're like old cars that are always needing new parts."

"Maria-José, how is it possible for one person to affect another by using objects that belong to that person?"

"When you wear a shirt or a shoe, the destiny of those objects becomes irrevocably linked to your own. The same way people project themselves onto everything around them, they also absorb into themselves the things around them. And they abandon a part of themselves into the objects. To have a part of someone in your possession means you have power over that person; you have, in a way, direct access to that person. One of your shirts or one of your shoes could represent you very well. And anything that's done to them will happen to you too."

"Are there any other ways of affecting someone?"

"The basic principle is always the same. You have to find something that symbolizes you well enough to work for or against you. Either an object that's lived in contact with you or an object that's made or found that resembles you. And then of course you need the help of the gods, since without them nothing can be done.

"People engaged in doing a work, whether it's good or evil, make use of a whole network of relationships to reach their goals. Several days ago a woman came to see me. She had problems. We talked, and bit by bit I came to realize that her spirit was like a tangled ball of wool. It was as if she had knots in her head which prevented her from seeing things clearly and from making the decisions which would have allowed her to advance.

"I gave her a ball of wool which was very tangled and asked her to unravel it. That was her work. If she could restore the real ball to order, I knew she'd be able to do it with the 'knots' in her mind."

"Do you often get involved with black magic — with Quimbanda?"

"My child, there's a lot more 'black work' than people usually believe. Quimbanda operates at night, in secret, in the forest or at the entrances to cemeteries. It hides, and it's impossible to track down. The priests of Quimbanda are often followers of our religion, sometimes even Mothers and Fathers of the Gods. Power has gone to their heads, they use the forces they have learned to master, but for evil ends.

"I fight Quimbanda with its own weapons. Exú is my ally too. I often ask him to undo the evil that he helped to bring about."

"How do you undo a work of Quimbanda?"

"I'll give you an example. Several months ago I had to undo a very serious Quimbanda work for the brother of one of our followers. This man works in an advertising agency, where he makes a good living. He had an important job, a new car, and a comfortable apartment in a modern building. Naturally his position caused envy all around him. Another employee of the same agency, who had a less important job, dreamed of taking his place. After working in vain behind the scenes, inside the agency, he decided to use more efficient, more radical methods. He knew a very famous *quimbandeira*, a priestess of Quimbanda. He went to see her, promising to pay her handsomely if she could get his colleague sick enough to make him quit his job and pass it on to him.

"When the case was brought to me, the work had been initiated more than two months before. The illness had taken root; the doctors gave the ailing man less than two months to live. One Friday at midnight I organized a special session in the terreiro. The ritual offerings were prepared, the altar was set up, and the ceremonial hall was filled with incense. One by one I approached each of the mediums who had entered a trance, but they saw nothing. The Quimbanda work had been extremely well executed. I couldn't find anything. The victim's brother, who was one of our followers, begged me to begin again. The next Friday I scheduled another session. Our mediums wore red to invoke the people of the Exús, the spirits of the cemeteries, and all the spirits that work for Quimbanda. I offered up blood and liquor. I summoned all the spirits who could come to our assistance. Finally an Exú descended upon one of our mediums and began to laugh convulsively. I asked him his name. Still laughing, he replied, 'Exú Furador' [literally, Exú the Piercer, Exú Who Makes Holes]. I asked him why he laughed like that. And he answered in his choppy, halting speech, 'Me? Why nothing, I just make little holes. . . .' I asked the victim's brother whether that made any sense to him, and he exclaimed, 'Yes! The doctors say that my brother has a perforated intestine — that's what the X-rays showed!' I questioned the spirit again. He gave me the name of the *quimbandeira*, and the man who had engaged her. He explained the motives behind the work. He laughed all the time and spoke very bad Portuguese, which made our conversation difficult. Finally I got angry and forced him to work for me to help me undo the work."

"What happened to the victim?"

"He got better, of course. But it took several weeks. Exú Furador undid the work he had begun and promised never to bother the brother of our follower again. On the day of his complete recovery we offered many gifts to all the spirits of Quimbanda. I could do nothing against the quimbandeira who had worked to bring about the spell, for she was strong enough to defend herself. As for the instigator of the work, the envious colleague, I later learned that he died in an automobile accident."

"Do you mean you killed him?"

"I never said anything of the sort."

"But you did say that spells could turn against those who originally cast them."

"That is true, but in this case I don't know anything. The man died. But why . . . is none of my business. All I did was undo a work of Quimbanda."

"You mentioned the existence of a whole people of Quimbanda. Then Exú isn't the only spirit who works for them?"

"No. Exú's the leader, but there are as many spirits of Quimbanda as there are spirits who work for good, the spirits of Umbanda. There are the people of the cemeteries, who are connected to the line of souls and to Omulú and even Iansã; there is the line of the caboclos quimbandeiros led by the *Pantera Negra*, the Black Panther; the people of the intersections; the obsessive spirits, and many many more. Each group has its specialty — some provoke sickness, others madness, others death."

"Up until now you've always avoided talking to me about Exú. Is that because he works for evil?"

"Exú doesn't work exclusively for evil. He works for anyone, anything, so long as he's handsomely rewarded and receives his share of liquor and cigars. The reason I hadn't spoken about him to you is because I wanted to avoid misunderstandings."

"Just now you said that Exú was the Devil."

"Exú can be the Devil, but he also accompanies Oxalá and Iemanjá and all the other gods. He is not a god like all the others. He has whatever face you want to give him. Last night you saw him with the features of the Devil, but he can also be the best of gods. . . .

"And then there are hundreds of Exús: Exú Pombagira, Exú

Death-Head, Exú of Cemeteries, Exú of Intersections, Exú Manguiera, Exú the Doorman. I don't know . . . he's got innumerable incarnations. But it would be wrong to think that he's only involved with evil. Quite the contrary, my child, quite the contrary."

"I don't understand. For example, which Catholic saint would you associate him with?"

"It all depends on which Exú you're talking about. In the Umbanda stories you'll often see red statuettes of devils with horns on their heads and a tail, holding a trident in their hands. This is the most common image of Exú you'll see. His wife, Pombagira, always accompanies him. She's also red and is shown with bare breasts and a twisted wicked smile. Most Brazilians think Exú is equivalent to Lucifer or Satan, the king of hell. You'll see him dressed in all sorts of different costumes: in black and red satin evening clothes and top hat, ready to attend a ball or pay a visit to the slum at the edge of town; or seated on a pile of skulls, holding a magician's wand or a deck of cards. Pombagira is deadly beautiful, she dances, covered with baubles and costume jewels. The outline of her body is visible through her transparent veils. She's extravagantly made up, and loves to lounge around in the doorways of nightclubs late at night. She's the gypsy, the woman of ill-repute. She likes men and liquor.

"But all these painted, decorated plaster casts are just symbolic representations of particular aspects of Exú and his wife. The true Exú — Elegbara or Bará — is made of rusted iron. He hides near the ground where no one can see him. He embodies godliness. Exú is not the Devil.

"Since he's the guardian of the ground and opener of paths,

Exú is sometimes associated with Saint Peter. And as the intermediary between human beings and the gods, and master of
the shells we use for divining, he's linked to the archangel
Gabriel. In some terreiros he's shown as Saint Bartholomew, in
others as Saint Paul. . . . As I said, he has many faces."

"What do you mean by 'Exú accompanies all the gods'?"

"Each god possesses one or more aspects of Exú. Thanks to
their Exús, the gods are able to realize their powers. Each god
has his or her special domain. Exú is the only one who feels at
home no matter where he is. He is the hyphen between gods.
He knows no barriers, no borders, no limits. Whenever a god
is unable to work, one of the Exús is employed.

"My mother used to say that Exú was the servant of the
gods. But I believe that he's much more than that. I don't
think the gods would have as many powers as they do if it
weren't for their Exús."

"How do you explain the fact that Exú is simultaneously on
the side of both good and evil?"

"But good and evil are human constructs, my child, values
created by us. The gods have never heard of them. *We* ask the
gods to work for good or evil ends, that is for *our* good, *our* ill.
But the gods are above all that. Our morality is of little concern to them."

"Are you saying that the followers of Macumba are above all
moral rules?"

"No, my son. The people of Macumba are the people of the
Faith. We call ourselves the children of the Law but the gods
aren't like us. We live in a society, and we have established
rules, both moral and otherwise, which are necessary if society
isn't going to disintegrate into pure chaos. But the society of

the gods isn't at all like human society. The gods have their rules too, but they aren't the same as ours. Because they don't perceive time the way we do, because their nature's different, because they don't exist on the same level we do. And maybe too because they're freer than we are. You know, the main concern of each species is its own survival. The gods need us to exist, and that's why they have to relate to us. But if somehow one day they could do without our bodies and our offerings — which luckily for us, I think is impossible — they'd drop us just like that, without the slightest hesitation."

"You say that human beings follow moral rules only for social ends, only out of a sense of obligation. Does that mean you don't believe human nature is fundamentally good?"

"I think that it's nicer to do good than evil. It brings more satisfaction. But as for the rest, I can only say that survival, self-interest and happiness are the primary factors."

"But I've seen you working alongside your mediums. You expend your energy selflessly to ensure the happiness of others; you've given your life to helping others, without the least reward for yourself, without the slightest personal gain."

"You're wrong, my child. What I do I do because it's impossible for me to do otherwise. I'm following my deepest nature, and that is my reward — to do what is most in harmony with myself. That's what I receive in exchange: the possibility of being who I am. And it's that possibility I *must* try to share."

"Then what if you were born a murderer or a thief?"

"I don't know, my child. I wasn't. But once again, be careful not to confuse true nature and imposed nature: what we truly are, and what our education and social background have turned us into. They are two different things."

"Do you think a person could be born with a fundamentally evil nature, completely independent of the social and cultural milieu?"

"Yes I do. But what you call 'evil' is still a social judgment. What you're really saying is 'evil toward others.' The evil person himself is actually just that — someone who's different from the majority. And our religion can help such people by teaching them to follow their nature without coming into conflict with others. How? By becoming an Exú, for example. By 'working' for us."

"Does Exú also descend? Does he have children who lend him their bodies?"

"Yes of course. I have two Exús in my terreiro. I had another one, but he was so furious about belonging to Exú that he preferred to deny it. He insisted I was wrong and that I had placed an evil god over his head. . . . He left the terreiro; he was ashamed of his god."

"How is it possible to be ashamed of your god?"

"You see, Exú has a very bad reputation. Everybody knows that he's a jokester, a gambler and a drinker, that he chases after women. . . . I forgot to tell you that Exú's also the god of fertility and fecundity. A long time ago he used to be shown not just with horns on his head, but with a huge erect penis. But Brazil is a Catholic country, so naturally such an obvious allusion to a god's sexuality gave him a terrible reputation.

"To be a child of Exú is very difficult. People laugh at you. Exú isn't like the other gods. Even his trances are different."

"Why? How does he reveal himself?"

"Well, he has a tendency to be exhibitionistic. To do more than everyone else. At the last festival we held in his honor one of his children stuck black and red candles — black and red are his colors — all over his body and raced up and down the terreiro blazing like a shop window. Also, his language isn't very clean, as you heard for yourself last night. He often expresses himself with 'dirty' words. Sometimes he pinches the pretty girls in the audience and makes all kinds of unsolicited remarks, puns and obscene gestures. That annoys people, but there's nothing we can do about it. It's his nature. Personally I have a great deal of respect for Exú."

"Are his different aspects related to his role in Quimbanda?"

"Yes and no. I think his importance in black magic stems mainly from the nature of some of his powers. He's closely linked to Omulú and Ogum. From Omulú he learned the secrets of disease and cemeteries. He inherited his knowledge of magic weapons and their uses from Ogum, the warrior god and patron of blacksmiths. So naturally he's in a good position to fight on behalf of disease and death, and to visit either of them on the designated victim. His main fault is he lets himself be corrupted so easily. All you have to do is offer him a bottle of beer or cachaça, or some good cigars, and he'll do anything you ask him to."

"You mentioned his wife, Pombagira; does she have the same powers as he does?"

"Yes. We say that she's his wife, but actually I think that's just a simple way of putting it. Exú doesn't have a sex, he *is* sex, both male and female. When we talk about his wife you have to understand we mean his female aspect. In any case Pombagira is even more terrible than he is. Exú is a jokester. Personally I find his sense of humor very appealing. I cannot make myself dislike him. Pombagira on the other hand is cold and implacable. Have you ever seen her smile? She never does — she sneers. When she strikes it's fatal. I think she enjoys killing people.

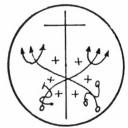

Graphic invocation of Pombagira:
Pombagira do cruzeiro

"Still she sometimes works for good ends too. She has followers, both at cemetery gates and in 'bad' neighborhoods — people who call on her because they know just how responsive she can be. She can solve all kinds of problems immediately before and after midnight which others have given up as completely hopeless. She appreciates the same offerings as Exú — liquor and strong cigars. She also likes some perfumes because she's a flirt. You have to flatter her, seduce her, and not blanch at her bad manners. She likes to shock. Show her that you notice her charm. And most of all never reject her, even if she becomes overbearing. When a daughter of the gods is possessed by Pombagira she makes eyes at all the men in the room. If that ever happens to you don't refuse her advances; play her game. It's not really a game after all. Pombagira has one trait that's sometimes embarrassing — she tells men the truth in the crudest terms, and a very loud voice. I've seen her reveal in public all the vices and flaws of one of our members; that he was cheating on his wife, that he was a miser, that he wore a wig. The man was red with shame and confusion. But he couldn't say a thing: Pombagira doesn't make her accusations lightly.

"She's the ally of women. She knows the secrets of femininity, childhood, pregnancy and love. If she thinks it's wise she can undo a pregnancy or make a woman fertile."

"Is it possible to practice black magic alone or do you always have to go through a Quimbanda priest?"

"Priests, no matter who they are, can only help people who are incapable of communicating with the gods by themselves. If you think you're capable of doing it, you can try to bring about someone's death all by yourself. But be careful. The forces you unleash have to strike somewhere. If you attack someone stronger than yourself, you can wind up being your own victim. You're also risking hurting someone who's completely innocent. The risks are great, my son, there are innumerable dangers."

"You told me that Exú was an 'opener of paths.' What sort of role does that imply?"

"In our religion everything we undertake begins with an offering to Exú. If the god isn't invoked at the beginning he will spoil the party, disturb the ceremony and ruin the work. That's what people say.

"In some terreiros they say that Exú thinks only about getting drunk, starting quarrels and breaking rules; that people have signed a pact with him, in order to keep him at a safe distance. The first sacrifice is always dedicated to him and in exchange he promises to keep out of the works we perform.

"Personally I think Exú is more than a simple party pooper. I believe all our invocations begin with him because he's the intermediary between us and the forces of Africa; because only he has the power to keep an equilibrium in our ceremonies.

"You see, the passage from the profane to the sacred isn't a simple one. Africa is far away. The gods don't always understand us. Exú stands on the border between the two worlds. He reigns in the uncertain zone that separates us from the gods. To sacrifice to him is to pay a fare, to buy a ticket to the land of the gods. For a few simple gifts Exú will bring us into contact with them. We pay for phone calls. Why should Exú work for nothing?

"And then he protects us. When our drums ring out all sorts of spirits hurry to join in the party, to use our bodies and receive our gifts. Some are desirable and some aren't. Exú the Doorman keeps away the evil spirits, who serve only to bring insanity and obsessions.

"On the days when we have sessions, the dancing doesn't start until the evening. But the ceremony itself starts in the morning, beginning with sacrifices. Exú is always served first. For him we kill a two-legged animal, for example a rooster. The sacrificer collects the blood in a bowl, separates the entrails and the flesh and cuts off the good pieces. The cooks of the gods prepare Exú's meal with strong spices and vegetables. Only then are the plates of the gods prepared and placed in the houses of the gods.

"Exú's food is placed with a glass of water and some candles at the intersection of two streets. We also light candles in front of his house. When Exú has eaten he announces to the gods that a feast is about to begin and that their children are ready to receive them, barefoot on the floor of the terreiro. Exú is our messenger, our courier."

"Why do you place his food at the intersection of two streets?"

"Exú is the master of intersections, since he is the god of all passageways. Intersections are rich in energy; they mark the place where the ways of different people cross, where space opens out in different directions.

"Whenever people have a request to make or want to receive the services of Exú, they always place their offerings at an intersection. You must have noticed the candles and presents dedicated to him all over the streets of our city. They correspond to the most divergent wishes."

"What do you have to do to get Exú on your side?"

"It all depends on what you're asking for. The offerings are simple: a few candles — the exact number depends on the nature of your request, liquor — either beer or cachaça, or whisky if you prefer, matches and cigars. . . . You go straight to the place that's been selected for your work, and carefully place your offerings on the ground. Then you begin to flatter the god (Exú is vain), assuring him that you've brought only the highest quality available for your offering. Then you ask him to intercede on your behalf."

"You speak to him aloud?"

"Yes, you want him to hear you. You say, for example, 'I love so-and-so, make her mine. . . ;' or 'I have money problems, can you solve them?' And then you say, 'If you help me, I'll give you more presents.' You light the candles, pour the beer into a glass, and open the bottle of liquor so he can serve himself. You thank him in advance and leave without looking back or turning around. All Brazilians know how to talk to Exú.

"There are two kinds of intersections, male and female. The first or male kind is formed by the crossing of two streets which continue (forming an X); the second is formed by a street which ends in another (forming a T). The female type is generally reserved for offerings to Pombagira. The hour is also important — it depends on whether it's before or after midnight. And the number of candles — even or odd.

"If you find a tree at the intersection the offering will be that much better received. Along with your gifts you can also offer money, red or black satin ribbons, flowers — roses or carnations — or a sacrificed or living animal. Some of our offerings can be very sophisticated, depending on what's being asked for. Of course not everything is requested at intersections. The gates of cemeteries, certain trees, certain stones, and the banks of a river are also places where Exú can be found."

"You told me that Exú was also master of thresholds."

"Yes. He's the protector of houses, but he should never be placed inside. Always outside, next to the main entrance. I don't know whether or not you've noticed a small niche with a small padlocked wooden door just outside our terreiro. That's Exú's house. All terreiros have to have at least one. Exú of the Threshold is a good protector.

"Deep down, Exú likes people. It's true he sometimes plays nasty tricks on them and laughs at their expense and makes fun of them. But he isn't necessarily wrong, is he? People are often ridiculous. Exú tries to exalt the parts of us that are most alive. He's very close to us. I would even go so far as to call him the most human of the gods."

"What do you mean by that?"

"People weren't made to be machines. Part of us is madness, a necessary madness Exú is the master of — this is the most creative part of us. It is the source of our evolution. Without Exú what would our lives be? Nothing but a monotonous repetition of passionless acts.

"Of course Exú is responsible for death — it was his idea. Also inequality, suffering, any number of other things that afflict us. Almost all our limitations come from him. That's why he's so often associated with the Devil, with the Fall, and with evil. But personally I don't believe in that story about a paradise we were once expelled from. All that only exists in our minds and just serves to explain and justify our little daily problems. Original sin is a bad excuse, my child. The origin of human troubles lies elsewhere. Besides, to believe that a perfect world existed once is a big weight to carry around, isn't it?

"To me the presence of Exú is reassuring. They say Exú is the Devil, that he's temptation. . . . But temptation is like a motor, a force pushing us forward. It's what's most dynamic in human beings.

"Of course Exú is like a clown. He's mischievous, a drunk, an instigator of quarrels and totally undisciplined. He's the black sheep of the gods. He does everything backwards. He takes pleasure turning the world inside out. But his disorder is necessary, because he is communication, exchanges, meetings. Exú, master of intersections, is at the center of space. Exú, master of divining shells, is at the center of time. Linked to the egums, the spirits of the dead, he stands between life and death; linked to Ossãe and to plants, he guards the doors of knowledge. He is the pivot of our religion, and the best ally of human beings — the essential point of communication between the sacred and profane. Exú is the mystery, the key to our religion. The other side of things."

"Do you mean that in Umbanda there is a whole esoteric doctrine that Exú is the guardian of?"

"No, my child. It's not that mystery I'm talking about. There are no secrets in our religion."

"Yet you mention secrets whenever you refer to plants, the dead, and particular powerful objects which, you say, are the force of the terreiro. . . ."

"Things are only secret to the degree that I refuse to speak to you about them . . . because you could never understand just through words. Even if you understood, your comprehension would be useless to you; even the contrary. You would have to be initiated and then, little by little, you would become familiar with the plants, the rituals for the dead, and the force of our most powerful objects. But there is nothing terribly mysterious about all that. It's nothing more than a long, laborious apprenticeship which you would undertake if that were your path. But all that is the use of things, not their mystery. Now what Exú holds is the key to the mystery of things, which no one can transmit."

"But isn't that the goal of initiation?"

"No, my child. Initiation, the preparation of the head of a medium, tries only to make possible the encounter with the mystery. During initiation we learn how to cross over to the 'other side' without risk, but not what the other side *is*."

"What do you mean by 'the other side'?"

"It is the other side of reality. Reality is two-fold, but the majority of people know only one of those sides, the one they've been taught. We Mothers of the Gods reveal the other side of things to our children, and accompany them there. You know for example that a tree is made of branches, leaves and roots. But we can tell you also what its power is, which god its spirit is related to, whether it has any powers and how they should be used.

"During initiation the medium learns how to be something other than what she's been told she was. She learns to be the vessel of a god, to cross over to the other side of things. I develop the other side of each medium's being, and she enters into the mystery."

"But if she crosses over into the mystery, doesn't she learn what the mystery is?"

"No. And that is never taught, it's not something that can be communicated. Once you cross over to the other side you're in a different reality. And when you return again to your normal state you've forgotten how to speak the language of the other reality."

"I don't understand. Don't the mediums speak the same language when they're in a trance as when they're not?"

"Didn't you notice that the first thing that changes when a medium crosses over to the other side is her way of speaking?"

"They speak in a choppy, distorted way, sometimes incoherently, using a lot of slang, and words from Umbanda and Africa. But it's still Portuguese."

"No, my son, it is not a pidgin language. It's another language, the language of the other reality. They don't deform words at random. They don't use a fanciful vocabulary because that's the only way they can speak. On the contrary. Because they're in a different world they speak a language adapted to that world. For that side of reality their language is perfectly coherent and correct.

"Sometimes the things a medium says during a trance are so obscure that an assistant has to translate. But really this translation is only an adaptation into the terms of our reality, of words from the other world where the medium is. It can never be the other reality itself, that's untranslatable."

"Then there is no means of communication between the world of gods and spirits and the human world?"

"That's precisely where Exú comes in. Only he can go from one side to another at will. Without him our religion truly would not exist. I believe that the gods understand us better than we understand them. Everything takes place through Exú's mediation. He links our daily profane world to the sacred land of the gods, to Africa. He is at once here and there; he is everywhere. He transmits our messages to the gods and summons them for us. He helps them reveal themselves to us. Sometimes he lies or purposely makes mistakes and does everything inside-out and upside-down, but how can we hold it against him? That's the source of both his charm and his humor."

"Do you mean to say he can't always be trusted? That it's a negative, destructive humor?"

"Only on the surface. Working with Exú always entails a certain risk. But that's because Exú is also the god of parties. His humor is a little like overturning our usual values. It's the art of letting one situation spill over into another, and so giving things a new dimension. . . ."

"You place a great importance on the distinction between the sacred and the profane. You always say that Africa is a sacred land. Is Africa Exú's domain?"

"Yes. Exú is the true black god. A god who will never age, since he's in continual motion. Maybe he symbolizes Africa. But Africa doesn't really belong to him. Africa is the domain of all the gods. It is the land of life, because it is the land of origins. Africa is the other world, my child. It is our force, our power."

"You constantly contrast Africa and Brazil. Do you mean to say that Brazil is devoid of strength?"

"Exú is the African soul, the true soul of all macumbeiros. Africa is our mother. All our strength comes from Africa."

"But what about the forces you've found here? You told me about that waterfall just outside the city. . . ."

"The energy and powers we find in Brazil also originate in Africa. There are secret, invisible links which bind us to our mother. They go under the ocean and bury themselves in the earth. You can't see them. But they nourish us with vital energy. Our soul is African; you mustn't forget that. We draw our life from that source."

"Don't you consider yourselves Brazilian? Aren't you perfectly assimilated here?"

"We're Brazilian and proud of it! That has nothing to do with it. We made Brazil. You're mistaken about the nature of this country. Brazil has many faces. It's Portuguese, it's Indian, but it's above all Black. Before they disappeared the Indians transmitted all their secrets to our slave ancestors, and it was the blacks who worked to keep them alive. It was the blacks' labor that built Brazil economically too. Brazil is African, my child, African."

"How does African energy reach you?"

"It's in the wind, in the sea. . . . Trees and forest plants seek it with their roots, in the soil. . . . And we do the same thing. Our limbs are like antennae, we capture it wherever we can. . . . In nature. . . . In our ceremonies we go barefoot so that we can feel the force of the earth rise into us, the force of the forest leaves that cover the terreiro floor. When we go to draw water for the Festival of Oxalá, we walk barefoot through the mountains for an hour. Shoes cut us off from the earth, my son. Their soles keep us from feeling and absorbing what the earth has to give us.

"People aren't nourished only through the mouth. We get hungry in the mind, our whole bodies cry out for energy. We need the living strength of nature. We need to eat with our feet, our hands, our skin. Everything you touch is as important as what you eat or breathe. To neglect this truth is to lay yourself open to impoverishment and disease."

"You speak of illness as an impoverishment. Don't you believe in microbes and germs?"

"All diseases come from the head. When the mind isn't strong enough, the body is open to disease. It lets itself be invaded by anything. When the mind is strong disease has no hold over the body. I'm not denying the existence of microbes. I'm simply saying that microbes attack us only when we place ourselves in a position of weakness. And that occurs when we forget nature and sacred space.

"People undervalue the things that are most essential. They look only at an object's utility and consider it neutral and inoffensive. But a hairdo or a way of dressing can affect your behavior."

"Is that why the mediums wear flowing white robes?"

"They're the clothes of our slave ancestors. What they wore on the plantations."

"One more tie to the past?"

"Yes, but that past is our identity. The gods recognize us more readily when we're wearing these clothes. When we wear them they can see us from far away. They aren't uniforms, but a sign of loyalty. And then their history gives them special powers. They're always sewn exactly as they were long ago — by hand, never by machine."

"But Maria-José, some of them are made of nylon. There wasn't any nylon long ago. . . ."

"The material isn't important. What counts, my child, is what we bring to it, the work, the 'manner.' "

"Isn't this attachment to the past a sign of conservatism? Isn't it a way of telling your followers to oppose all forms of change — to oppose progress?"

"You're talking politics, aren't you?"

"Yes. Does Umbanda have a specific political attitude or role in Brazil?"

"We don't get involved in politics. I can't speak in the name of all terreiros, but personally I never try to influence the political consciousness of my followers. You reproach us for a certain conservatism. Others have accused us of aiding or encouraging opposition movements — maybe because we were underground for so long. But that was long ago. In any case I think both interpretations show a basic misunderstanding of our role. Our only task is to help people to live better, to feel better."

"But isn't the absence of political identification a revealing attitude?"

"My son, I think our ambitions are higher than that. Most of all we want our followers to become conscious of themselves. I told you I believe the most essential thing is to discover your own deep nature and learn to live it fully. I think that if people become better, they are taking a bigger step forward than if they seek to change the people around them. Individual progress leads more surely to group progress than vice versa. If all people realized themselves fully, politics would no longer exist; everybody would be happy.

"This is our political struggle: to teach people to fulfill themselves. We don't incite to inaction, on the contrary. We want our followers to break out of their chains and become who they really are.

"Now on a purely religious level Umbanda — which, don't forget, is still a very young religion, since the first terreiros were established at the beginning of this century — is right at the height of its development. I always speak of our mother Africa, since she is our strength. But it is less a historic reference than it is the magic source of our powers."

"Maria-José, would you go to Africa if you could?"

"It would be a great honor. . . ."

"Do you think the trip would bring you new powers?"

"You know, the gods always come when I call them."

"How do you imagine Africa?"

"Africa is like a virgin forest. A reservoir of forces. It is nature, sacred space."

"You always contrast virgin nature with inhabited land. Is this like the distinction you make between profane Brazil and sacred Africa?"

"I don't understand."

"It seems to me that when you speak of Africa you're talking most of all about nature uncontaminated by the hands of man. . . ."

"But that's what Africa is. . . . Yes, a long time ago we were blacks in exile in Brazil; today we're human beings in exile in cities. Africa is a virgin land which has never known the evils of man. It's the land from before the exile. I don't know how to put it. . . . It's everything the intelligence can't grasp, strength in its raw state. . . ."

"Then do you believe that people should flee the oppression of cities?"

"I never said that. Cities respond to a need; you can't simply flee them. In fact, we keep trying to get closer to them. They stand for guaranteed jobs, social progress, a better life. Cities are good for us.

"Except that the transition from nature to city isn't without its losses. It requires compensation. Cities suck more energy from us than they give. So people in cities have more need of the gods and of terreiros, of powerful objects and places."

"I was astonished when I first came to Brazil to see Macumba ceremonies taking place in the downtown areas of large cities like Rio de Janeiro and Saõ Paulo. I was confused when I heard drums beating in front of steel and concrete sky-scrapers — and when I found that the most modern, fast-paced life went hand in hand with trances and candles. I've heard that Macumba is essentially an urban phenomenon, that there are more centers in the cities than in the countryside."

"I don't know. But that sounds right to me, doesn't it?"

"Doesn't having modern medical centers nearby and the contact with new scientific discoveries put a damper on the development of your religion?"

"My child, very educated, cultured people can also believe in the gods. Our religion isn't behind the times; it is oriented toward the future. We encourage scientific progress, just as we encourage all efforts that benefit humanity.

"Our followers are not illiterate. We have professors, doctors and lawyers among the members of our terreiro. They watch television, read newspapers and go to the movies. They're up on what's going on in the world. They don't feel our religion is incompatible with modern life. In fact I think it has never been so needed as it is today. Maybe we're the religion of the future. . . . Science . . . now science has limits, my child. It's obvious it's not sufficient; it alone cannot resolve all our problems."

"You say that there are doctors who belong to your terreiro. Do they ever refer patients to you?"

"Of course. They've seen with their own eyes the results we obtain. They know our possibilities and they know their own. Our methods differ but they're not mutually exclusive. Sometimes they ask us to complete a treatment by initiating someone or performing a work. And they never regret it."

"Has the inverse ever occurred? That is, have you ever advised one of your followers to consult a doctor?"

"No, that has never happened. I haven't needed to up to this point. You see, there are things that science can't and never will fight effectively, human diseases which it cannot cure because they don't fall under its jurisdiction. Today you can find pills to help you sleep, eat, feel better, calm down or forget yourself. But it's not these things that will bring us equilibrium. People who think they will find answers in pills have a very poor opinion of themselves. The problem lies elsewhere, my child. People need life. The dimensions of life make us suffer, and all our problems stem from that. What our religion offers to its children is the expansion of their life possibilities — the possibility of living out their deepest nature."

"What do you think is the future of Macumba?"

"The number of our followers continues to grow. New terreiros are opening every year. We have more and more need of
the gods. And the gods, my son, are not about to abandon
us. . . ."

EPILOGUE

Daughters at a ceremony.

A Mother of the Gods visits a neighboring terreiro.

EPILOGUE

WINTER and summer, night falls early in Rio de Janeiro. The sun sinks behind the twin peaks of Dos Irmãos, the *maté* vendors leave the beaches, and the glass and marble buildings of the residential areas, Ipanema and Leblon, fill with the glow of a thousand reflections.

On the other side of the city, beyond the interminable tunnel which leads to the Zona Norte, at the end of a narrow alley in the midst of houses painted pink or pistachio, in the terreiro of Maria-José, a group of women huddles over the body of a black rooster. The blood of the bird has been collected in a bowl. Selected pieces of its meat will be cooked and offered to the gods. In a small room the mediums are changing from their street clothes to the ceremonial white robes worn by daughters of the gods. Fresh leaves have been spread over the floor of the ceremonial hall, and vases have been filled with fresh-cut flowers.

Maria-José receives me with a smile. I tell her of my plan to assemble our conversations into a book. I show her my notes and the photographs I have taken of her. She is especially interested in the photographs, and asks to have copies of two of them. I explain the basic outline of the book, the form it will take, and discuss the main themes with her. I ask for her opinion.

"It's strange. . . . What you say sounds right to me. But I don't know. I don't recognize my voice. Did we really talk that much? You wrote everything down. . . . Books aren't all that useful."

We are sitting in the kitchen. Women bustle around the stoves. Maria-José shows them the photographs, which they pass around in a circle.

"What will the people who read it think of me? I'm not a professor. I'm not a philosopher. And philosophy has nothing to do with our religion. On the contrary. Thought kills life, my son. Takes the strength out of things. Ask our followers. They can't explain what they do or feel. But it's not necessary to explain everything. Many ideas run through my mind, but I only believe the things I've actually experienced. Our religion is practiced, not studied. So I don't understand your book. It's like a song you only know the words to. And I told you — the rhythms are the essential thing."

She hands me a cup of coffee. "You'd need colors, smells, feelings. And music — what will you say about our drums? No book can speak as well as they do."

Maria-José is sitting upright on the edge of her chair. She taps my knee with an ironic look. I try to justify myself. I explain to her that the book is not intended to be read by Brazilian macumbeiros, but by a foreign audience which is as ignorant of her religion as I was when I first came to Brazil. My arguments do not seem to convince her. She shakes her head. She reminds me that my coffee must be getting cold and repeats, "Books are not very useful. Because you've learned to respect our religion, maybe even believe in it, you try to justify it, to explain it all. To give an order and a reason to everything you've heard. You make me sound like a sage. You find complicated meanings in the things I say. But I'm just an ignorant Mother of the Gods of a small terreiro in the suburbs. . . ."

She smiles. "I'm very flattered to be quoted in your book. Our followers will make sure that everybody in the neighborhood knows my picture's going to be published. You'll have to send me a copy of your book when it comes out. . . . The Mothers of the Gods of terreiros near here will be very surprised to see it."

She gets up. "You'll always be welcome here." She wishes me a peaceful journey under Oxalá's protection. She gives me her blessing and, not without majesty, stretches out her hand for me to kiss.

Rio de Janeiro-Paris
1972-1976

GLOSSARY

Agogô: double metal bell which is hit with an iron stick to make the gods descend.

Axé: object containing great spiritual force, which has been sanctified by immersion in herbal baths and the blood of sacrificial animals; also, the force itself.

Axogum: Initiate in charge of sacrificing animals.

Azeite de dendê: Palm oil; often used in the preparation of certain offertory dishes.

Babalaô: priest of the cult of Ifa; divine. High religious authority of Candomblé (see below).

Batuque: term for Macumba in the state of Rio Grande do Sul.

Buzios: cowrie shells used for divining; the oracle.

Caboclos: originally, Indian *mestizos*; now used to designate Indian spirits who "work" in the forest and know the secrets of plants and herbs.

Camarinha: small room within the *terreiro* which is reserved for initiates; this is the room in which novices live throughout the initiation period.

Cambone: assistant to the Mother; sacrificer of animals (see *axogum*).

Candomblé: extremely traditional Afro-Brazilian cult, native to the state of Bahia.

Catimbó: term for Umbanda in northeast Brazil.

Culto de Naçâo: Cult of the Nations, Afro-Brazilian cult in Rio Grande do Sul.

Despacho: Macumba offering, generally of a sacrificial animal.

Dijina: holy name received by those who have just been initiated.

Ebane: term for a *yaõ* (see below) who has reached a higher level of spirituality.

Egums: souls or spirits of the dead:

Engira: Corruption of *gira* (to turn); dance, or Macumba session.

Eré: an infantile trance.

Exú: god of intersections, of magic, etc.; intermediary between human beings and the gods.

Figa: ornamental fist with the thumb between the middle and index fingers; worn to ward off evil.

Iansã: goddess of the River Niger; goddess of the wind; consort of Xangô in Macumba's pantheon; associated with St. Barbara or Joan of Arc.

Ibejis: twins, sacred children; patrons of doctors and pharmacists; associated with Saints Cosmas and Damian.

Iemanjá: goddess of salt water; Our Lady of the Sea; identified with the Virgin Mary.

Maconha: *cannabis indica*, a form of marijuana sometimes used in Macumba ceremonies.

Macumbeiro: believer in Macumba.

Mae de Santo: Mother of the Gods; high priestess of Macumba and head of a *terreiro*.

Oba: ministers, apostles of Xangô; honorary title.

Odum: pattern of cowrie shells used in divination.

Ogan: male assistant to a Mother of the Gods.

Ogãs: skilled musicians initiated to play the drums.

Ogum: warrior god; associated with St. George.

Omulú: god of sickness and cemeteries; associated with St. Lazarus.

Orixá: literally, master of the head; god or goddess; deity.

Ossãe: god of sacred plants and herbs.

Oxalá: god of the sky and universe; associated with Jesus Christ.

Oxossi: god of the hunt and the forest; associated with St. Sebastian.

Oxum: goddess of the River Oxum in Africa; goddess of fresh water. Controls all feminine activity; associated with Saint Catherine.

Pajelança: Afro-Brazilian cult native to the Amazon.

Peji: inner sanctuary of the *terreiro*, where the ritual accessories of the gods and goddesses are kept and special offerings are made.

Pemba: ritual chalk used in drawing *pontos riscados* (see below).

Pombagira: wife of Exú.

Ponto cantado: Macumba chant.

Ponto riscado: magic diagram used to summon god or goddess.

Pretos Velhos: black ancestor spirits who incarnate wisdom and experience.

Quimbanda: black magic.

Quimbandeira: priestess of Quimbanda.

Saravá: ritual greeting.

Terreiro: Macumba temple or place of worship.

Umbanda: another word for Macumba, particularly used in Rio de Janeiro.

Xangô: god of fire or thunder. Symbolizes all masculine forces; associated with Saint Jerome.

Yaõ: recently initiated medium; a "bride" of the gods.

CITY LIGHTS PUBLICATIONS

Eberhardt, Isabelle. THE OBLIVION SEEKERS
Eidus, Janice. VITO LOVES GERALDINE
Fenollosa, Ernest. CHINESE WRITTEN CHARACTER AS A MEDIUM FOR POETRY
Ferlinghetti, L. ed. CITY LIGHTS POCKET POETS ANTHOLOGY
Ferlinghetti, L., ed. ENDS & BEGINNINGS (City Lights Review #6)
Ferlinghetti, L. PICTURES OF THE GONE WORLD
Finley, Karen. SHOCK TREATMENT
Ford, Charles Henri. OUT OF THE LABYRINTH: Selected Poems
Franzen, Cola, transl. POEMS OF ARAB ANDALUSIA
García Lorca, Federico. BARBAROUS NIGHTS: Legends & Plays
García Lorca, Federico. ODE TO WALT WHITMAN & OTHER POEMS
García Lorca, Federico. POEM OF THE DEEP SONG
Garon, Paul. BLUES & THE POETIC SPIRIT
Gil de Biedma, Jaime. LONGING: SELECTED POEMS
Ginsberg, Allen. THE FALL OF AMERICA
Ginsberg, Allen. HOWL & OTHER POEMS
Ginsberg, Allen. KADDISH & OTHER POEMS
Ginsberg, Allen. MIND BREATHS
Ginsberg, Allen. PLANET NEWS
Ginsberg, Allen. PLUTONIAN ODE
Ginsberg, Allen. REALITY SANDWICHES
Goethe, J. W. von. TALES FOR TRANSFORMATION
Gómez-Peña, Guillermo. THE NEW WORLD BORDER
Harryman, Carla. THERE NEVER WAS A ROSE WITHOUT A THORN
Heider, Ulrike. ANARCHISM: Left Right & Green
Herron, Don. THE DASHIELL HAMMETT TOUR: A Guidebook
Herron, Don. THE LITERARY WORLD OF SAN FRANCISCO
Higman, Perry, tr. LOVE POEMS FROM SPAIN AND SPANISH AMERICA
Jaffe, Harold. EROS: ANTI-EROS
Jenkins, Edith. AGAINST A FIELD SINISTER
Katzenberger, Elaine, ed. FIRST WORLD, HA HA HA!: The Zapatista Challenge
Kerouac, Jack. BOOK OF DREAMS
Kerouac, Jack. POMES ALL SIZES
Kerouac, Jack. SCATTERED POEMS
Kerouac, Jack. SCRIPTURE OF THE GOLDEN ETERNITY
Lacarrière, Jacques. THE GNOSTICS
La Duke, Betty. COMPAÑERAS
La Loca. ADVENTURES ON THE ISLE OF ADOLESCENCE
Lamantia, Philip. BED OF SPHINXES: SELECTED POEMS
Lamantia, Philip. MEADOWLARK WEST
Laughlin, James. SELECTED POEMS: 1935–1985
Laure. THE COLLECTED WRITINGS
Le Brun, Annie. SADE: On the Brink of the Abyss
Mackey, Nathaniel. SCHOOL OF UDHRA
Masereel, Frans. PASSIONATE JOURNEY
Mayakovsky, Vladimir. LISTEN! EARLY POEMS
Mrabet, Mohammed. THE BOY WHO SET THE FIRE
Mrabet, Mohammed. THE LEMON
Mrabet, Mohammed. LOVE WITH A FEW HAIRS
Mrabet, Mohammed. M'HASHISH

Murguía, A. & B. Paschke, eds. VOLCAN: Poems from Central America
Murillo, Rosario. ANGEL IN THE DELUGE
Nadir, Shams. THE ASTROLABE OF THE SEA
Parenti, Michael. AGAINST EMPIRE
Parenti, Michael. DIRTY TRUTHS
Pasolini, Pier Paolo. ROMAN POEMS
Pessoa, Fernando. ALWAYS ASTONISHED
Peters, Nancy J., ed. WAR AFTER WAR (City Lights Review #5)
Poe, Edgar Allan. THE UNKNOWN POE
Porta, Antonio. KISSES FROM ANOTHER DREAM
Prévert, Jacques. PAROLES
Purdy, James. THE CANDLES OF YOUR EYES
Purdy, James. GARMENTS THE LIVING WEAR
Purdy, James. IN A SHALLOW GRAVE
Purdy, James. OUT WITH THE STARS
Rachlin, Nahid. THE HEART'S DESIRE
Rachlin, Nahid. MARRIED TO A STRANGER
Rachlin, Nahid. VEILS: SHORT STORIES
Reed, Jeremy. DELIRIUM: An Interpretation of Arthur Rimbaud
Reed, Jeremy. RED-HAIRED ANDROID
Rey Rosa, Rodrigo. THE BEGGAR'S KNIFE
Rey Rosa, Rodrigo. DUST ON HER TONGUE
Rigaud, Milo. SECRETS OF VOODOO
Ross, Dorien. RETURNING TO A
Ruy Sánchez, Alberto. MOGADOR
Saadawi, Nawal El. MEMOIRS OF A WOMAN DOCTOR
Sawyer-Lauçanno, Christopher, transl. THE DESTRUCTION OF THE JAGUAR
Scholder, Amy, ed. CRITICAL CONDITION: Women on the Edge of Violence
Sclauzero, Mariarosa. MARLENE
Serge, Victor. RESISTANCE
Shepard, Sam. MOTEL CHRONICLES
Shepard, Sam. FOOL FOR LOVE & THE SAD LAMENT OF PECOS BILL
Smith, Michael. IT A COME
Snyder, Gary. THE OLD WAYS
Solnit, Rebecca. SECRET EXHIBITION: Six California Artists
Sussler, Betsy, ed. BOMB: INTERVIEWS
Takahashi, Mutsuo. SLEEPING SINNING FALLING
Turyn, Anne, ed. TOP TOP STORIES
Tutuola, Amos. FEATHER WOMAN OF THE JUNGLE
Tutuola, Amos. SIMBI & THE SATYR OF THE DARK JUNGLE
Valaoritis, Nanos. MY AFTERLIFE GUARANTEED
Vanden Broeck, André. BREAKING THROUGH
Veltri, George. NICE BOY
Waldman, Anne. FAST SPEAKING WOMAN
Wilson, Colin. POETRY AND MYSTICISM
Wilson, Peter Lamborn. SACRED DRIFT
Wynne, John. THE OTHER WORLD
Zamora, Daisy. RIVERBED OF MEMORY